SICILY TRAVEL
GUIDE

**Discover The Magic Of Sicily, Uncover Its
Hidden Gems, Top Attractions, Dining,
Nightlife & Activities. Your Insider's Guide
To The Island**

Chris West

TABLE OF CONTENT

Useful apps and websites

Conclusion

Introduction

Welcome to Sicily

Sicily is a land of contrasts, where ancient ruins coexist with modern cities, and rugged coastlines give way to verdant valleys. Its strategic location in the middle of the Mediterranean has made it a melting pot of cultures and a crossroads of civilizations for thousands of years. Over the centuries, Sicily has been ruled by Greeks, Romans, Byzantines, Arabs, Normans, Spaniards, and Italians, among others, each leaving their mark on the island's culture, art, and architecture.

Today, Sicily is a vibrant and dynamic region that offers visitors a unique blend of ancient history, stunning landscapes, and delicious cuisine. From the bustling streets of Palermo to the quiet countryside of the interior, Sicily has something for everyone. Whether you are interested in exploring the island's rich cultural heritage, relaxing on a sandy beach, or hiking in a nature reserve, Sicily has it all.

Sicily's history is reflected in its art and architecture, with magnificent temples, theaters, and monuments dotting the landscape. The Valley of the Temples in Agrigento is one of the most famous archaeological sites in the world, while the Cathedral of Monreale near Palermo is a masterpiece of Norman architecture. Meanwhile, the island's rugged coastline and volcanic landscapes provide a stunning backdrop for outdoor activities such as hiking, swimming, and sailing.

Sicilian cuisine is also famous around the world, with its emphasis on fresh, seasonal ingredients and bold flavors. From the seafood of the coastal regions to the hearty meat dishes of the interior, Sicilian cuisine is a feast for the senses. And of course, no trip to Sicily would be complete without a taste of the island's famous desserts, such as cannoli, cassata, and granita.

Whether you are a history buff, a foodie, or an outdoor enthusiast, Sicily has something to offer. So come and explore the hidden gems of this fascinating island, and experience the magic of Sicily for yourself.

Why Visit Sicily?

Rich History: Sicily has a long and fascinating history that dates back thousands of years. It has been ruled by various civilizations, from the Greeks and Romans to the Normans and Arabs. Each of these cultures has left its mark on the island, creating a unique blend of art, architecture, and traditions that can be seen in Sicily's cities, museums, and ancient ruins.

Beautiful Landscapes: Sicily is home to a diverse range of natural landscapes, from the rugged mountains of the interior to the sandy beaches of the coast. One of the most iconic natural features of Sicily is Mount Etna, an active volcano that dominates the island's skyline. The Aeolian Islands, a UNESCO World Heritage Site, are also worth visiting for their stunning beaches, clear waters, and volcanic scenery.

Delicious Cuisine: Sicilian cuisine is known for its fresh ingredients, bold flavors, and unique combinations. Some of the most famous dishes include arancini (fried rice balls), pasta alla norma (pasta with eggplant and tomato sauce), and cannoli (a sweet pastry filled with ricotta cheese). Sicily is also a major producer of wine, with several renowned wine regions throughout the island.

Cultural Heritage: Sicily has a rich cultural heritage that can be seen in its art, architecture, and festivals. The island's capital, Palermo, is home to several historic churches, palaces, and museums, while the ancient Greek city of Syracuse boasts one of the largest and best-preserved ancient theaters in the world. Sicily is also famous for its vibrant festivals, such as the Feast of Saint Agatha in Catania and the Infiorata in Noto.

Warm Hospitality: Sicilian people are known for their warm hospitality and friendly nature. Visitors to Sicily can expect to be greeted with open arms and treated like family, whether they are staying in a small bed and breakfast or a luxury hotel. The locals are also known for their love of life, which is reflected in their lively festivals, delicious food, and vibrant culture.

Beaches: Sicily is blessed with some of the most beautiful beaches in the Mediterranean. With crystal-clear waters, fine golden sands, and scenic views, the beaches in Sicily are perfect for a relaxing day out. Some of the most popular beaches in Sicily include San Vito lo Capo, Mondello, and the Vendicari Nature Reserve.

Art and Architecture: Sicily has a rich history of art and architecture, with a number of stunning buildings and monuments that are well worth visiting. The island is home to several UNESCO World Heritage Sites, including the ancient Greek ruins of Agrigento, the Baroque towns of Val di Noto, and the Norman cathedrals of Palermo. Visitors can also enjoy exploring the island's historic towns and villages, with their narrow streets, charming squares, and picturesque architecture.

Adventure Activities: Sicily is a great destination for adventure lovers, with plenty of opportunities for hiking, cycling, and water sports. Visitors can explore the island's rugged mountains, nature reserves, and coastal areas on foot or by bike, or try their hand at activities such as windsurfing, snorkeling, and scuba diving. Mount Etna is also a popular destination for hiking and offers spectacular views of the island from its summit.

Local Festivals and Events: Sicily is home to a number of colorful and vibrant festivals and events throughout the year, including the Carnival of Acireale, the Almond Blossom Festival in Agrigento, and the Festival of Saint Rosalia in Palermo. These events offer a unique insight into the island's rich culture and traditions, and are a great way to experience the warm hospitality of the Sicilian people.

In conclusion, Sicily is a destination that offers something for everyone, from its rich history and culture to its stunning natural landscapes, delicious cuisine, and warm hospitality. Whether you are interested in exploring ancient ruins, relaxing on a beautiful beach, or trying new and exciting foods, Sicily has it all.

Packing list

When planning a trip to Sicily, it's important to pack appropriately for the climate and the activities you plan to do. Here is a comprehensive packing list to help you prepare for your trip:

Clothing: Sicily has a warm climate, especially during the summer months, so pack light, breathable clothing made from natural fibers such as cotton or linen. Shorts, sundresses, and t-shirts are suitable for daytime, while long pants and light jackets are useful for cooler evenings. Don't forget to pack comfortable shoes for sightseeing and hiking, as well as a swimsuit and beachwear for trips to the beach.

Sun protection: The Sicilian sun can be strong, so it's important to pack sun protection such as a hat, sunglasses, and sunscreen with a high SPF. Consider bringing a sun umbrella or beach tent for extra shade.

Travel documents: Make sure to pack all the necessary travel documents such as your passport, visa (if required), and travel insurance. It's also a good idea to make photocopies of your important documents and keep them separate from the originals.

Electronics: Don't forget to bring your camera, phone, and charger, as well as any other electronic devices you may need. It's a good idea to bring a travel adapter for any electrical outlets that may differ from those in your home country.

Medications: If you take any medications, be sure to bring enough for the duration of your trip. It's also a good idea to bring a copy of your prescription, as well as any over-the-counter medications you may need, such as pain relievers and antihistamines.

First aid kit: Pack a small first aid kit with essentials such as band-aids, antiseptic cream, and insect repellent. If you plan to do any hiking or outdoor activities, consider adding items such as blister pads and anti-inflammatory medication.

Cash and credit cards: It's always a good idea to have a mix of cash and credit cards for your trip. Make sure to notify your bank and credit card company of your travel plans to avoid any issues with card usage.

Travel guide and maps: Bring a travel guide and maps of the area you plan to visit, as well as any language guides you may need.

Snacks and water: Pack some snacks and a refillable water bottle to keep you hydrated and energized throughout the day.

Backpack or daypack: A backpack or daypack is useful for carrying all your essentials while you're out and about exploring.

Travel pillow and blanket: If you have a long flight or train ride to Sicily, a travel pillow and blanket can help make your journey more comfortable.

Lightweight rain jacket: Although Sicily is mostly sunny and warm, it's still a good idea to pack a lightweight rain jacket or umbrella in case of sudden rain showers.

Travel-sized toiletries: To save space in your luggage, pack travel-sized toiletries such as shampoo, conditioner, toothpaste, and body wash. Don't forget to pack a small towel as well.

Comfortable day bag: Bring a comfortable day bag or backpack for carrying your essentials while exploring the cities and towns of Sicily.

Smart casual outfit: Although Sicily is generally a casual destination, it's a good idea to bring a smart casual outfit for dining at higher-end restaurants or attending special events.

Adapter and converter: Sicily uses the Europlug Type C and Type F sockets, so be sure to bring an adapter and converter if necessary.

Insect repellent: Sicily can have a mosquito problem during the summer months, especially in more rural areas, so bring insect repellent to avoid bites.

Portable charger: Bring a portable charger to ensure that your phone and other devices always have enough battery power.

Swimsuit cover-up: A swimsuit cover-up is useful for trips to the beach or pool, and can also double as a lightweight dress or top.

Travel insurance documents: Make sure to bring your travel insurance documents, including contact information for emergency assistance, in case of any unexpected incidents or accidents.

By packing these items, you can ensure that you're well-prepared for your trip to Sicily, no matter what activities you plan to do or what surprises may arise. Don't forget to pack light and leave room in your luggage for souvenirs and gifts to bring back home. With its stunning landscapes, rich history, and delicious cuisine, Sicily is a destination that you'll never forget, and with the right preparation, you'll be able to fully enjoy all that it has to offer.

Best time to visit

Sicily is a beautiful and diverse island located in the Mediterranean Sea, with a rich history, stunning beaches, and delicious cuisine. The best time to visit Sicily depends on your preferences, as the island offers something for everyone all year round. Here's a guide to help you decide when to plan your trip to Sicily.

Summer (June - August): Summer is the peak tourist season in Sicily, with long, hot days and warm nights. This is the perfect time to enjoy the island's stunning beaches, swim in the clear blue waters, and indulge in delicious gelato. However, the high temperatures can be intense, with average temperatures hovering around 30°C (86°F), and crowds can be overwhelming in popular tourist spots. It's also the most expensive time to visit, with prices for accommodation and activities at their highest.

Spring (March - May): Spring is a great time to visit Sicily, with mild temperatures, fewer crowds, and lower prices. The island comes alive with blooming flowers and greenery, making it a great time to explore the countryside and historic sites. The weather is ideal for hiking and cycling, and the sea is starting to warm up, making it possible to take a dip in some of the more sheltered bays. However, be aware that the sea may still be too cold for swimming in some areas.

Autumn (September - November): Autumn is another great time to visit Sicily, with pleasant temperatures, fewer tourists, and lower prices. The weather is still warm enough for swimming and sunbathing, and the sea is at its warmest during this time of year. The countryside is also a great place to explore during the autumn months, with vineyards and olive groves at their most picturesque. However, be aware that some attractions and restaurants may close earlier than during the peak season.

Winter (December - February): Winter is the off-season in Sicily, with cooler temperatures and shorter days. However, it's still possible to enjoy the island's rich history and culture, as well as its delicious cuisine. The winter months are a great time to explore the island's cities and towns, with fewer tourists and lower prices. The ski resorts on Mount Etna also open during this time of year, offering a unique winter sports experience. However, it's important to note that some restaurants and attractions may be closed during the winter months.

In conclusion, the best time to visit Sicily depends on your interests and preferences. Each season offers its own unique experiences and attractions, so it's important to consider what you want to see and do during your trip. Whether you're looking for a relaxing beach vacation, an active outdoor adventure, or a cultural immersion, Sicily has something for everyone all year round.

Geography and Climate

Sicily is a diverse and beautiful island, offering a variety of landscapes and natural wonders. The island's geography is characterized by three mountain ranges that run from east to west, as well as numerous valleys and coastal plains. The Nebrodi Mountains are located in the northeast and are the highest range on the island, with peaks reaching over 1,800 meters. The Madonie Mountains are located in the center of the island and are known for their rugged terrain and stunning views. The Peloritani Mountains are located in the northeast and form a natural barrier between Sicily and the Italian mainland.

In addition to the mountains, Sicily is also home to a number of beautiful beaches, rocky coastlines, and quaint fishing villages. The island's coastline stretches for over 1,000 kilometers and offers a variety of scenery, from sandy beaches to rocky cliffs. Some of the most popular beaches in Sicily include San Vito lo Capo, Mondello, and Cefalù.

The island's interior is home to numerous nature reserves and parks, offering visitors the chance to explore the island's diverse flora and fauna. The Nebrodi Regional Park is the largest nature reserve on the island and is home to a variety of wildlife, including wild boar, foxes, and eagles. The Zingaro Nature Reserve is located on the western coast of the island and is known for its crystal-clear waters and rocky cliffs.

Sicily's climate is typically Mediterranean, with mild winters and hot summers. However, the weather can vary greatly depending on the location and time of year. The western side of the island is generally wetter than the eastern side, with more rainfall in the winter months. The summer months can be very hot, with temperatures often reaching over 30 degrees Celsius. It's important to pack accordingly and to stay hydrated when exploring the island during the summer months.

Overall, Sicily's diverse geography and climate offer visitors a wealth of opportunities to explore and experience the island's natural beauty and wonders.

History and Culture

Sicily is a beautiful and historic island located in the Mediterranean Sea, just off the coast of Italy. It has a rich and diverse history that spans thousands of years, with influences from various civilizations such as the Greeks, Romans, Normans, Arabs, and Spanish. Sicily's history and culture are deeply intertwined, and visitors to the island can experience this unique blend of traditions, architecture, and cuisine.

History of Sicily:

Sicily's history dates back to prehistoric times, with evidence of human settlements dating back to the Paleolithic era. Over the centuries, the island was ruled by various civilizations, including the Greeks, Romans, Byzantines, Arabs, Normans, Spanish, and Italians. Each of these civilizations left their mark on the island, shaping its culture, architecture, and way of life.

The Greeks, who colonized the island in the 8th century BC, had a profound influence on Sicilian culture. They founded several important cities, including Syracuse and Agrigento, and introduced the concept of democracy to the island. The Romans, who conquered Sicily in the 3rd century BC, also played a significant role in shaping the island's history, building roads, aqueducts, and other infrastructure.

In the medieval period, Sicily was ruled by the Normans, who brought their own unique style of architecture and culture to the island. They also established a vibrant court culture, which attracted scholars, artists, and intellectuals from across Europe. The Arabs, who ruled Sicily in the 9th and 10th centuries, also had a significant influence on the island, introducing new crops such as citrus fruits, almonds, and rice.

Culture of Sicily:

Sicilian culture is a unique blend of traditions, customs, and influences from various civilizations.

The island is known for its vibrant and colorful festivals, delicious cuisine, stunning architecture, and rich artistic heritage.

One of the most famous aspects of Sicilian culture is its cuisine. Sicilian food is known for its bold flavors, fresh ingredients, and unique blend of culinary traditions. Some of the island's most famous dishes include arancini, pasta alla Norma, and cannoli. Sicily is also famous for its wines, particularly Marsala, a sweet fortified wine that is produced in the western part of the island.

Sicilian architecture is also a testament to the island's rich cultural heritage. From ancient Greek temples to medieval castles and Baroque churches, Sicily is home to a wealth of architectural treasures. Some of the most famous examples of Sicilian architecture include the Valley of the Temples in Agrigento, the Cathedral of Monreale, and the Palazzo dei Normanni in Palermo.

Sicily is also known for its vibrant festivals and celebrations. The island is home to several festivals throughout the year, celebrating everything from the harvest season to religious holidays. Some of the most famous festivals include the Feast of Saint Agatha in Catania, which honors the city's patron saint, and the Infiorata in Noto, where locals create intricate flower carpets on the streets.

In conclusion, Sicily's rich history and culture make it a fascinating destination for visitors. From its ancient Greek temples to its medieval castles and stunning Baroque churches, the island is a testament to the diverse civilizations that have called it home over the centuries. Visitors can immerse themselves in Sicilian culture by sampling the island's delicious cuisine, attending its vibrant festivals, and exploring its architectural treasures.

People and Language

Sicily is an island located in the Mediterranean Sea and is the largest island in Italy. It is known for its rich cultural heritage, stunning landscapes, and unique cuisine. The island has a diverse population, and the people of Sicily are a fascinating mix of different ethnicities and cultures.

The majority of people in Sicily are of Italian descent, but there are also significant numbers of people with Greek, Arab, and Spanish ancestry.

Sicily has been inhabited by many different civilizations over the centuries, and each has left its mark on the island's culture and people.

Sicilian people are known for their hospitality, warmth, and generosity. They are proud of their heritage and are happy to share their traditions and customs with visitors. Family is very important in Sicilian culture, and many families live in close proximity to each other, often in the same house or apartment building.

The official language of Sicily is Italian, but many Sicilian people also speak Sicilian, which is a Romance language with Arabic, Greek, and Spanish influences. Sicilian is not an official language, but it is widely spoken throughout the island, especially in rural areas. Sicilian has many dialects, and each region of the island has its own unique dialect and accent.

Sicilian cuisine is famous around the world for its delicious flavors and unique ingredients. The food in Sicily is heavily influenced by the island's history and its position in the Mediterranean Sea. Some of the most popular dishes in Sicilian cuisine include arancini (deep-fried rice balls), pasta alla norma (pasta with eggplant, tomato sauce, and ricotta salata), and cannoli (a dessert made with sweetened ricotta cheese and pastry).

Sicilian music is also an important part of the island's culture, and there are many traditional music festivals and events throughout the year. Sicilian folk music is characterized by its use of stringed instruments such as the mandolin and guitar, and it often tells stories of love, hardship, and life on the island.

In conclusion, the people and language of Sicily are a fascinating mix of different cultures and traditions. Sicilian people are known for their warmth and hospitality, and the island's cuisine, music, and culture are a reflection of its rich history and diverse population. A visit to Sicily is an opportunity to immerse yourself in a unique and vibrant culture and experience the warmth and generosity of the Sicilian people.

Food and Drink

Sicily is known for its rich and diverse culinary tradition that reflects its rich cultural history and influences from various civilizations that have passed through the island. From street food to fine dining, Sicily has something to offer for everyone's taste buds. Here's a detailed content on food and drink in Sicily:

Street food: Sicilian street food is famous throughout Italy, and it's a must-try for anyone visiting the island. Some of the popular street foods in Sicily include arancini, which are fried rice balls stuffed with meat, cheese, and tomato sauce; panelle, which are fritters made from chickpea flour and served in a sandwich; and sfincione, which is a type of pizza topped with onions, tomatoes, anchovies, and cheese.

Seafood: Sicily is an island surrounded by the Mediterranean Sea, and seafood plays a prominent role in its cuisine. From swordfish to sardines, Sicily has a wide range of seafood dishes to offer. Some of the popular seafood dishes in Sicily include spaghetti alle vongole, which is spaghetti with clams in a white wine sauce; pesce spada alla siciliana, which is swordfish cooked with tomatoes, capers, and olives; and sarde a beccafico, which is sardines stuffed with breadcrumbs, pine nuts, and raisins.

Pasta: Sicilian cuisine has a wide range of pasta dishes, from the famous pasta alla norma to the lesser-known busiate con pesto trapanese. Pasta alla norma is a dish made with eggplant, tomatoes, basil, and ricotta salata cheese. Busiate con pesto trapanese is a pasta dish made with busiate, a traditional Sicilian pasta shape, served with a pesto made from almonds, basil, garlic, and tomatoes.

Desserts: Sicilian desserts are famous throughout Italy, and for a good reason. From cannoli to cassata, Sicilian desserts are rich, sweet, and full of flavor. Cannoli are fried pastry shells filled with sweetened ricotta cheese and candied fruit. Cassata is a sponge cake layered with ricotta cheese, candied fruit, and marzipan, and soaked in liqueur.

Wine: Sicily is a significant wine-producing region in Italy, and it's home to several indigenous grape varieties. Some of the popular wines produced in Sicily include Nero d'Avola, a full-bodied red wine, and Grillo, a white wine that pairs well with seafood dishes.

In addition to the above, Sicily has several traditional dishes and specialties that are worth trying, including caponata, a sweet and sour eggplant relish, and pasta con le sarde, a pasta dish made with sardines, fennel, and pine nuts. When it comes to drinks, Sicily has several popular beverages, including limoncello, a sweet lemon liqueur, and amaro, a bitter liqueur made from herbs and spices.

Cheese: Cheese lovers will not be disappointed with the range of cheeses available in Sicily. Pecorino Siciliano is a sheep's milk cheese that's often grated over pasta dishes or eaten as a snack. Caciocavallo is a semi-hard cheese that's often grilled or melted over bread. And then there's ricotta, a soft, creamy cheese that's used in many Sicilian dishes, including cassata and cannoli.

Fruits and Vegetables: Sicily's warm climate and fertile soil make it an ideal region for growing a variety of fruits and vegetables. Oranges, lemons, and other citrus fruits are abundant, and you'll find them used in everything from salads to desserts. Tomatoes, eggplants, and peppers are also common ingredients in many Sicilian dishes.

Coffee: Italians are famous for their coffee, and Sicily is no exception. Espresso is the most common type of coffee served in Sicily, and it's often enjoyed with a sweet pastry, such as a cannolo or a brioche. If you're feeling adventurous, try ordering a caffè corretto, which is an espresso with a shot of liquor, usually grappa or amaro.

Aperitivi: Aperitivi, or pre-dinner drinks, are an important part of Sicilian culture. Aperitivi are usually light and refreshing drinks that are served before dinner to stimulate the appetite. Some of the popular aperitivi in Sicily include Aperol Spritz, Campari Spritz, and Negroni.

Olive Oil: Sicily is one of the largest producers of olive oil in Italy, and the island's olive oil is known for its high quality and fruity flavor. Sicilian olive oil is used in many Sicilian dishes, including salads, pasta dishes, and grilled meats.

In conclusion, Sicilian cuisine is a celebration of the island's rich cultural history and fertile land. From street food to fine dining, Sicily has a wide range of dishes and drinks to offer, and you're sure to find something that will satisfy your taste buds. So, when you're in Sicily, make sure to indulge in the local specialties and experience the island's culinary delights.

Festivals and Events

Sicily is a vibrant and colorful region of Italy, famous for its stunning landscapes, delicious cuisine, and rich cultural heritage. One of the best ways to experience the spirit of Sicily is to attend one of its many festivals and events, which celebrate everything from religious traditions to local produce and folklore. Here are some of the most popular festivals and events in Sicily:

Feast of Saint Agatha: The Feast of Saint Agatha is one of the most famous and important religious festivals in Sicily, held in honor of the patron saint of Catania. The festival takes place every February, and includes processions, parades, and religious ceremonies, as well as plenty of food and drink.

Infiorata di Noto: The Infiorata di Noto is a stunning flower festival held in the town of Noto every May. The streets of the town are decorated with intricate floral carpets made from thousands of flower petals, creating a stunning and colorful display.

Festival of the Almond Blossom: The Festival of the Almond Blossom is held every February in Agrigento, and celebrates the arrival of spring with parades, music, and plenty of delicious almond-based treats.

Feast of Santa Rosalia: The Feast of Santa Rosalia is held in Palermo every July, and celebrates the city's patron saint with a huge street party, fireworks, and a procession of the saint's statue through the streets.

Cous Cous Fest: The Cous Cous Fest is a popular food festival held every September in San Vito lo Capo, showcasing the best of Sicilian and North African cuisine, with a particular focus on cous cous dishes.

Festino di Santa Rosalia: The Festino di Santa Rosalia is another festival held in honor of the patron saint of Palermo, and takes place in July. The festival includes processions, music, and traditional Sicilian food, as well as a spectacular fireworks display.

Sicily Jazz Festival: The Sicily Jazz Festival is a popular music festival held every summer, featuring a range of jazz and blues performers from around the world. The festival takes place in a number of venues across the island, including outdoor amphitheaters and historic palazzos.

Festival of the Sea: The Festival of the Sea is held every August in the town of Cefalù, and celebrates the town's close ties to the sea with boat races, fishing competitions, and plenty of seafood-based dishes.

Feast of the Black Madonna: The Feast of the Black Madonna is held in the town of Tindari every September, and celebrates the town's famous statue of the Black Madonna. The festival includes processions, music, and traditional Sicilian food, as well as a reenactment of the legendary miracle of the Black Madonna.

When planning your visit to Sicily, it's a good idea to research the various festivals and events taking place during your stay, as they can provide a unique and memorable insight into the local culture and traditions. Many festivals are free to attend, and offer a great opportunity to mingle with locals and experience the lively atmosphere of Sicilian celebrations.

In addition to the events listed above, there are also many smaller local festivals and fairs taking place throughout Sicily, celebrating everything from wine and cheese to art and music. Some of the most popular local festivals include the Feast of San Giovanni in Modica, the International Puppet Festival in Palermo, and the Grape Harvest Festival in Pachino.

When attending festivals and events in Sicily, it's important to be respectful of local traditions and customs. Dress modestly and conservatively, especially for religious events, and be mindful of local etiquette when interacting with locals. It's also important to be aware of your belongings, as festivals can be crowded and pickpocketing can occur.

Overall, festivals and events are a wonderful way to experience the vibrant culture and traditions of Sicily. From colorful floral displays to lively music and dancing, the festivals of Sicily offer a unique and unforgettable glimpse into the heart and soul of this beautiful region.

Chapter 2: Planning Your Trip

When planning a trip to Sicily, there are several factors to consider to ensure that your visit is enjoyable and hassle-free. This chapter covers everything you need to know to plan your trip, including when to go, how to get there, getting around, accommodations, and budgeting.

When to Go

Sicily has a Mediterranean climate, with mild winters and hot summers. The best time to visit Sicily depends on your preferences, as the island has something to offer all year round.

The shoulder seasons of April to June and September to November are considered the best times to visit Sicily. During these months, the weather is pleasant, and the crowds are thinner. Temperatures range from 15°C to 25°C (59°F to 77°F), making it perfect for outdoor activities and sightseeing.

July and August are peak tourist seasons in Sicily, and temperatures can soar up to 40°C (104°F). During this time, the beaches are crowded, and accommodations can be more expensive. However, it's a great time to experience the island's vibrant festivals, such as the Feast of St. Agatha in Catania or the Infiorata flower festival in Noto.

If you're a winter sports enthusiast, then January and February are the best months to visit Sicily. The island's highest peak, Mount Etna, offers skiing and snowboarding opportunities during these months. The temperature drops to around 5°C (41°F) in coastal areas, and it can get colder in the mountains.

In addition to weather and crowds, it's also essential to consider other factors when planning your trip to Sicily. These factors include events and festivals, budget, and personal preferences.

Events and Festivals:

Sicily is known for its vibrant and colorful festivals that take place throughout the year. If you're interested in experiencing these events, it's worth considering when to visit Sicily. For example, the Feast of Santa Rosalia in Palermo takes place in July, while the Festival of Saint Lucy in Syracuse takes place in December.

Budget:

Another essential factor to consider when planning your trip to Sicily is your budget. The cost of accommodations, transportation, and attractions can vary depending on the time of year you visit. Generally, peak tourist season (July and August) is the most expensive time to visit, while the shoulder seasons (April to June and September to November) are more affordable.

Personal Preferences:

Ultimately, the best time to visit Sicily depends on your personal preferences. If you prefer warm weather and crowded beaches, then July and August may be the best time for you. If you prefer mild temperatures and fewer crowds, then the shoulder seasons may be ideal. Consider your interests and travel style to determine the best time to visit Sicily.

Overall, the best time to visit Sicily depends on a variety of factors. By considering weather, crowds, events, budget, and personal preferences, you can choose the time of year that works best for you. Whenever you decide to visit, Sicily is sure to offer a memorable and enriching travel experience.

How to Get There

Air Travel:

Sicily has two major international airports, Falcone-Borsellino Airport in Palermo and Catania-Fontanarossa Airport in Catania. These airports are serviced by many airlines from various cities across Europe and beyond. From the airport, you can take a taxi, bus or train to your final destination.

Sea Travel:

Sicily has several ports, with regular ferries from mainland Italy and neighboring islands. The most popular ports are Palermo, Catania, Messina, Trapani, and Milazzo. There are also ferry services from Naples, Genoa, Civitavecchia, and Salerno. If you're traveling from Malta, you can take a ferry from Valletta.

Land Travel:

You can also reach Sicily by land via Italy. There are two ways to cross from mainland Italy to Sicily: by train or car ferry. The train journey involves boarding a train in Rome or Naples and taking it to either Villa San Giovanni or Reggio Calabria. From there, you can board a car ferry to Messina in Sicily. The car ferry is a popular option for those traveling by car or motorcycle. You can drive your vehicle onto the ferry in Villa San Giovanni or Reggio Calabria and cross the Strait of Messina to Sicily.

Internal Transportation:

Once you arrive in Sicily, there are several transportation options to get around the island. The most common modes of transport are buses and trains, which connect major cities and towns. The bus network is comprehensive, affordable, and reliable, with different operators serving different routes. The train network is also efficient, and trains run regularly between major cities. Taxis are available in cities and towns, but they can be expensive. Car rental is another option for those who prefer to explore the island at their own pace. Many car rental companies operate on the island, and it's advisable to book in advance, especially during peak season.

In summary, getting to Sicily can be done by air, sea, or land, depending on your preference and location. Once you arrive, there are several transportation options to explore the island, including buses, trains, taxis, and car rental. It's essential to plan your transportation in advance to ensure a smooth and enjoyable trip.

Getting Around

Public transportation in Sicily is reliable and affordable, making it a popular option for travelers. Buses and trains connect major cities and towns, and there are also regional and local routes that serve more remote areas. However, it's important to note that public transportation in Sicily can be slow and infrequent, and schedules may not always be reliable.

If you prefer more flexibility and independence, renting a car is a great option. Car rental agencies are available at most airports and major cities, and prices are generally reasonable. However, driving in Sicily can be challenging, especially for inexperienced drivers. The roads are often narrow, winding, and steep, and the local driving style can be aggressive.

When driving in Sicily, it's important to be aware of the rules of the road. Speed limits are posted in kilometers per hour, and the limit is 50 km/h (31 mph) in cities and 90 km/h (56 mph) on highways. Seatbelts are mandatory, and it's illegal to use a mobile phone while driving. It's also important to note that parking in cities and towns can be difficult, and parking spaces are often limited.

Another option for getting around in Sicily is by taxi. Taxis are widely available in cities and towns, and fares are regulated by the government. However, taxi fares can be expensive, especially for longer distances.

Finally, if you're looking for a more unique and adventurous way to explore Sicily, consider renting a bike or a scooter. This is a great way to experience the island's stunning scenery and landscapes up close. However, it's important to be aware of the risks involved, especially when riding on busy roads.

Getting around in Sicily requires careful consideration of the various transportation options available. Whether you choose public transportation, car rental, taxi, or a more adventurous option like biking or scootering, it's important to be aware of the challenges and risks involved. By planning ahead and taking the necessary precautions, you can ensure that your travels in Sicily are safe and enjoyable.

Accommodations

Sicily offers a wide range of accommodations to suit every budget and preference. From luxury hotels and villas to budget-friendly hostels and guesthouses, there are plenty of options to choose from. Some popular areas to stay include Palermo, Taormina, and Syracuse.

Hotels and Resorts

Sicily has no shortage of high-end hotels and resorts, particularly in popular tourist destinations such as Taormina and Palermo. Many of these properties offer luxurious amenities such as spas, swimming pools, and beach access. Prices for these accommodations can be steep, particularly during peak season, but they are well worth the splurge for those seeking an indulgent vacation.

Guesthouses and B&Bs

Guesthouses and bed and breakfasts (B&Bs) are a popular option for travelers seeking a more authentic and affordable experience. Many of these properties are family-run and offer personalized service and local insights. Prices for these accommodations vary depending on location and amenities, but they tend to be more affordable than hotels.

Hostels

Sicily also has several hostels scattered throughout the island, particularly in larger cities such as Palermo and Catania. Hostels are a great option for budget-conscious travelers and those seeking a social atmosphere. Many hostels offer dormitory-style rooms, as well as private rooms and shared bathrooms.

Vacation Rentals

Vacation rentals such as apartments and villas are becoming increasingly popular in Sicily, particularly for longer stays or for families or groups traveling together. Many of these properties offer fully equipped kitchens and other amenities that make them feel like a home away from home.

It's important to book your accommodations in advance, particularly during peak season. Most properties can be booked online, but it's a good idea to read reviews and compare prices before making a decision. Many properties offer discounts for longer stays or for booking directly through their website.

In summary, Sicily offers a wide range of accommodations to suit every budget and preference. From luxury hotels and resorts to budget-friendly hostels and vacation rentals, there are plenty of options to choose from. By researching and booking in advance, you can find the perfect accommodation for your Sicilian vacation.

Budgeting and Money Matters

Sicily is generally an affordable destination, with lower prices than other parts of Italy. However, it's essential to budget for transportation, accommodations, meals, and attractions. Here are some tips to help you plan your budget:

Transportation: Public transportation in Sicily is affordable, with buses and trains connecting major cities and towns. A one-way bus ticket costs around €1.50-€3, while a train ticket between cities can cost between €5 and €20, depending on the distance. Car rental prices vary depending on the season and rental duration, with rates starting from €20 per day.

Accommodations: Accommodations in Sicily range from luxury hotels and villas to budget-friendly hostels and guesthouses. The average cost of a mid-range hotel room is around €70-€120 per night, while budget hostels and guesthouses can cost around €20-€50 per night.

Meals: Sicilian cuisine is known for its fresh seafood, pasta dishes, and traditional street food. Dining out can be affordable, with prices ranging from €8-€20 for a main course at a mid-range restaurant. Street food and casual dining options can cost between €2-€8 per dish.

Attractions: Sicily offers a wide range of attractions, from ancient ruins and historical sites to beautiful beaches and natural reserves. The cost of admission varies depending on the attraction, with fees ranging from €5-€20 per person.

Miscellaneous expenses: Other expenses to consider include travel insurance, visa fees (if applicable), and souvenirs. It's always a good idea to have some extra cash on hand for unexpected expenses or emergencies.

When it comes to money matters, the official currency in Sicily is the Euro (EUR). ATMs are widely available in cities and towns, and credit cards are accepted at most hotels, restaurants, and shops. However, it's advisable to carry some cash, especially when visiting more remote areas.

Overall, budgeting for a trip to Sicily requires careful planning and research. By taking the time to budget for transportation, accommodations, meals, attractions, and miscellaneous expenses, you can ensure that your trip is enjoyable and stress-free.

Chapter 3: Exploring Sicily's Top Attractions

Palermo and the Surrounding Area

Palermo is the capital of the Italian island of Sicily, and one of the most fascinating cities in Italy. With its mix of different cultures and influences, Palermo has a unique character that sets it apart from other Italian cities. The city's history dates back to the 8th century BC, and it has been ruled by a variety of different powers over the centuries, including the Greeks, Romans, Arabs, Normans, and Spanish. Each of these civilizations has left its mark on Palermo's architecture, culture, and traditions.

Must-See Attractions in Palermo

The Cathedral of Palermo: This iconic landmark is one of the most important religious sites in Sicily. The cathedral was built in the 12th century and has undergone several renovations since then. The cathedral features a unique blend of architectural styles, including Norman, Gothic, Baroque, and Neoclassical.

The Palatine Chapel: Located within the Norman Palace, the Palatine Chapel is a masterpiece of Norman architecture and is known for its stunning mosaics, which cover the walls, ceiling, and floor. The chapel was built in the 12th century and is one of the most important examples of Norman art in Sicily.

The Quattro Canti: The Quattro Canti, or Four Corners, is a Baroque square in the heart of Palermo. The square features four palaces, each representing one of the four seasons, and is a popular spot for tourists to take photos.

The Teatro Massimo: The Teatro Massimo is the largest opera house in Italy and is known for its stunning architecture and acoustics. The opera house was built in the late 19th century and has hosted some of the most famous operas in the world.

The Capuchin Catacombs: This eerie and fascinating attraction is a must-visit for anyone interested in history and macabre artifacts. The catacombs contain the mummified remains of over 8,000 people, including monks, nobles, and everyday citizens.

The Mercato di Ballarò: This vibrant and bustling market is a must-visit for foodies and anyone interested in experiencing the local culture of Palermo. The market is known for its fresh produce, seafood, and street food, and is a great place to sample traditional Sicilian cuisine.

The Church of San Giovanni degli Eremiti: This beautiful church is a blend of Arab-Norman architecture and is known for its distinctive red domes. The church was built in the 12th century and is one of the most important examples of Arab-Norman architecture in Palermo.

The Zisa Castle: This stunning castle was built in the 12th century and is a prime example of Arab-Norman architecture. The castle features beautiful gardens, fountains, and a small museum.

The Palermo Botanical Gardens: Located on the outskirts of Palermo, the botanical gardens are a beautiful and peaceful oasis in the heart of the city. The gardens feature over 12,000 species of plants, including many rare and exotic species.

These are just a few of the many must-see attractions in Palermo. Whether you're interested in history, architecture, food, or culture, Palermo has something to offer everyone. Plan your trip to Palermo today and experience the beauty and charm of this stunning Sicilian city.

Excursions and Day Trips from Palermo

Monreale and Cefalù: A popular day trip from Palermo is to visit the nearby towns of Monreale and Cefalù. Monreale is known for its stunning cathedral, which is considered one of the finest examples of Norman architecture in Sicily. Cefalù is a charming seaside town, famous for its picturesque beaches, ancient ruins, and historic center.

Segesta and Erice: Another popular day trip from Palermo is to visit the ancient ruins of Segesta and the hilltop town of Erice. Segesta is home to a well-preserved Greek temple and a theater that dates back to the 5th century BC. Erice is a medieval town perched on a hilltop, offering stunning views of the surrounding countryside.

Agrigento and the Valley of the Temples: A longer day trip from Palermo is to visit the town of Agrigento and the Valley of the Temples, a UNESCO World Heritage Site. The Valley of the Temples is home to some of the best-preserved Greek temples in the world, including the Temple of Concordia, the Temple of Hera, and the Temple of Zeus.

Mount Etna: For those who enjoy outdoor activities, a trip to Mount Etna, the tallest active volcano in Europe, is a must-do excursion from Palermo. Visitors can hike around the base of the volcano or take a cable car to the summit for stunning views of the surrounding landscape.

Zingaro Nature Reserve: The Zingaro Nature Reserve is a beautiful protected area located on the western coast of Sicily, known for its crystal-clear waters, rugged cliffs, and abundant wildlife. Visitors can hike along the coastal trails, swim in secluded coves, and enjoy a picnic lunch in the shade of the trees.

Madonie Mountains: The Madonie Mountains are a stunning range of peaks located just a short drive from Palermo. The area is home to picturesque medieval towns, charming farmhouses, and scenic hiking trails, as well as a range of local produce, including cheese, honey, and wine.

Whether you're interested in ancient ruins, picturesque towns, or stunning natural landscapes, there is something for everyone within easy reach of Palermo. With a little bit of planning and some adventurous spirit, you can easily explore the many wonders of this beautiful region of Sicily.

Dining and Shopping in Palermo

Palermo, the capital city of the Italian island of Sicily, is a hub of culture, history, and gastronomy. The city offers visitors a wide range of dining and shopping options, from traditional Sicilian cuisine to modern boutiques and local markets. Here's a guide to some of the best places to eat and shop in Palermo:

Dining:

Antica Focacceria San Francesco: This historic eatery, founded in 1834, is a must-visit for anyone looking to try traditional Sicilian street food. Specialties include arancini (fried rice balls), panelle (chickpea fritters), and of course, the classic Sicilian snack of focaccia.

Trattoria del Pesce Fresco: This cozy seafood restaurant is a favorite among locals and visitors alike, offering fresh seafood dishes made with locally sourced ingredients. The menu changes daily depending on what's available at the market, but highlights include spaghetti alle vongole (clam spaghetti) and pesce spada (swordfish).

Osteria dei Vespri: For a more upscale dining experience, head to Osteria dei Vespri, located in a historic palazzo in the heart of Palermo's old town. The menu features contemporary twists on classic Sicilian dishes, such as duck with orange and fennel, and sea urchin linguine.

Il Gelato di San Crispino: After a meal, cool off with a scoop of gelato from Il Gelato di San Crispino. This artisanal gelateria uses only the finest ingredients, including local fruits and nuts, to create creamy and delicious gelato flavors.

Shopping:

Mercato di Ballarò: One of Palermo's most famous markets, Mercato di Ballarò is a bustling hub of activity, with vendors selling everything from fresh produce to clothing and souvenirs. It's a great place to experience the lively atmosphere of Palermo's street markets and pick up some local treats to take home.

Via Roma: For upscale shopping, head to Via Roma, one of Palermo's main shopping streets. Here you'll find a mix of high-end designer boutiques, as well as more affordable Italian brands such as Benetton and Calzedonia.

Artigianato Siciliano: For unique souvenirs and gifts, check out Artigianato Siciliano, a store specializing in locally made handicrafts and artisanal products. You'll find everything from handmade ceramics and jewelry to gourmet food products like olive oil and wine.

Vucciria Market: Another famous Palermo market, Vucciria is known for its colorful displays of fruits and vegetables, as well as its vendors selling fresh fish, meat, and cheese. It's a great place to stock up on ingredients for a picnic or cooking at home.

Overall, Palermo offers a wealth of dining and shopping options for visitors, from traditional Sicilian street food to upscale dining experiences and local markets selling handmade products. Whether you're looking for souvenirs to take home or a memorable meal, Palermo has something to offer everyone.

Agrigento and the Valley of the Temples

Introduction to Agrigento:

Agrigento is located on the southwestern coast of Sicily and is home to the famous Valley of the Temples, one of the most impressive collections of ancient Greek ruins in the world. The city itself is also worth exploring for its baroque architecture, beautiful churches, and charming historic center.

Agrigento's history and culture:

Founded as a Greek colony in the 6th century BC, Agrigento was an important center of commerce and culture for centuries. The city was later conquered by the Romans, Arabs, and Normans, leaving a rich cultural heritage visible in its architecture and art. Today, Agrigento is a UNESCO World Heritage Site and a popular destination for history and culture enthusiasts.

The Valley of the Temples - an overview:

The Valley of the Temples is a vast archaeological park that contains the remains of several ancient Greek temples, including the Temple of Concordia, the Temple of Juno, and the Temple of Hercules. The temples were built between the 6th and 5th centuries BC and are some of the best-preserved ancient Greek ruins in the world.

Highlights of the Valley of the Temples:

The Temple of Concordia is one of the best-preserved ancient temples in the world, and is widely considered to be one of the most beautiful. Built in the 5th century BC, the temple is an excellent example of the Doric style of Greek architecture. The temple's impressive columns, pediments, and friezes are adorned with intricate carvings and sculptures, including depictions of mythological scenes and figures.

The Temple of Juno, located on the highest point in the Valley, offers stunning views of the surrounding landscape. The temple, which was built in the 5th century BC, is dedicated to the goddess Juno, and is another excellent example of Doric architecture. The temple is also notable for its unique construction, which features a sloping base that follows the contours of the hill upon which it is built.

The Temple of Hercules, although only partially preserved, is notable for its massive columns and imposing appearance. Built in the 6th century BC, the temple was dedicated to the legendary hero Hercules, and is one of the oldest structures in the Valley of the Temples. The temple's remaining columns, which are over 8 meters tall, are among the largest and most impressive of any ancient Greek temple.

Other notable attractions in the Valley of the Temples include:

- The Temple of Olympian Zeus, which was once the largest temple in the Valley, and featured a massive statue of Zeus that was among the largest in the ancient world
- The Tomb of Theron, an ancient burial site that is adorned with intricate carvings and decorations
- The Sanctuary of Demeter and Persephone, which was once a religious center dedicated to the goddesses of the harvest and the underworld

Visitors to the Valley of the Temples can also explore the nearby Archaeological Museum of Agrigento, which features a collection of artifacts and exhibits related to the history and culture of the region. The museum's collection includes ancient coins, pottery, sculptures, and other artifacts, many of which were recovered from the ruins of the Valley of the Temples and other nearby sites.

Tips for visiting the Valley of the Temples:

To make the most of your visit to the Valley of the Temples, it's important to plan ahead and come prepared. Here are some tips to keep in mind:

- Wear comfortable shoes, as there is a lot of walking involved.
- Bring plenty of water, especially in the summer months when temperatures can be high.
- Consider hiring a guide to learn more about the history and significance of the temples.
- Take your time to explore the different temples and soak up the atmosphere.
- Be respectful of the ancient ruins and follow any rules or guidelines posted on site.

Agrigento and the Valley of the Temples are must-see destinations for anyone interested in ancient history and culture. With its impressive ruins, beautiful architecture, and rich cultural heritage, Agrigento offers a glimpse into Sicily's fascinating past. By following these tips and recommendations, you can make the most of your visit to this incredible destination.

Syracuse and the Southeast Coast

Syracuse, or Siracusa in Italian, is a historic city located on the southeast coast of Sicily. It was once one of the most powerful cities in the ancient Greek world and is now a UNESCO World Heritage Site. The city boasts a rich history, culture, and architecture, making it one of the most popular destinations in Sicily.

Syracuse's history and culture

Syracuse has a fascinating history dating back to the 8th century BC when it was founded by the ancient Greeks. The city grew in importance over the centuries, becoming one of the most important cities in the ancient Greek world. It was also an important center of art and culture during the Renaissance period.

Today, visitors can explore Syracuse's history and culture through its many archaeological sites and museums. The city's main attractions include the Greek Theater, the Ear of Dionysius, the Roman Amphitheater, and the Archaeological Park of

Neapolis. The city also has several museums, including the Paolo Orsi Archaeological Museum and the Regional Gallery of Palazzo Bellomo.

Must-see attractions in Syracuse

In addition to its historical and cultural attractions, Syracuse also has several beautiful natural landmarks. One of the city's most popular attractions is the island of Ortigia, which is the historical center of Syracuse. Here, visitors can explore narrow alleys, charming piazzas, and impressive buildings such as the Cathedral of Syracuse and the Fountain of Arethusa.

Other must-see attractions in Syracuse include the Catacombs of San Giovanni, the Church of Santa Lucia alla Badia, and the Basilica of Santa Maria delle Colonne. Visitors can also take a boat tour of the nearby Plemmirio Marine Nature Reserve to see beautiful landscapes and marine life.

Excursions and day trips from Syracuse

Syracuse is also an excellent base for exploring the surrounding area. Visitors can take day trips to nearby towns and attractions such as the Baroque town of Noto, the Vendicari Nature Reserve, and the Cavagrande del Cassibile Nature Reserve. Visitors can also explore the nearby town of Avola, which is known for its almond trees and wine production.

Recommendations for dining and shopping in Syracuse

Syracuse is known for its excellent seafood and traditional Sicilian cuisine. Visitors can enjoy fresh seafood dishes, such as swordfish and tuna, at the many seafood restaurants in Ortigia. The city also has several traditional markets, such as the Ortigia Market and the Market of Santa Lucia, where visitors can purchase local produce, spices, and handicrafts.

Syracuse is a fascinating destination on the southeast coast of Sicily that offers a unique blend of history, culture, and natural beauty. Visitors can explore the city's many archaeological sites, museums, and natural landmarks, as well as take day trips to nearby towns and attractions. With its excellent dining and shopping options, Syracuse is a must-visit destination for anyone traveling to Sicily.

Mount Etna and the Northeast Coast

Mount Etna is one of the most popular attractions in Sicily, as it is one of the most active volcanoes in the world and a UNESCO World Heritage Site. The Northeast Coast of Sicily is also a popular destination due to its beautiful coastline and picturesque towns.

Mount Etna's History and Culture

Mount Etna has been active for over 500,000 years and has shaped the landscape and culture of the surrounding area. The volcano has had a significant impact on the local agriculture, as the rich volcanic soil is ideal for growing grapes, citrus fruits, and olives. Mount Etna has also played a role in Sicilian mythology and folklore, with many stories and legends associated with the volcano.

Activities and Attractions on Mount Etna

- Hiking: There are many hiking trails on Mount Etna that offer spectacular views of the volcano and the surrounding countryside.
- Cable Car and Jeep Tours: For those who prefer a less strenuous way to see the volcano, there are cable car and jeep tours that take visitors to various parts of the volcano.
- Visiting Craters: There are several craters on Mount Etna that visitors can explore, including the Bove Valley, Valle del Leone, and Valle del Bove.
- Wine Tasting: The area around Mount Etna is home to some of Sicily's best wineries, and visitors can enjoy wine tastings and tours of the vineyards.
- Skiing: During the winter months, Mount Etna is a popular destination for skiing and other winter sports.

Other Attractions on the Northeast Coast

- The town of Taormina is a must-visit destination on the Northeast Coast, with its ancient Greek theater and stunning views of the coastline.

- The Alcantara Gorge is a natural wonder that is worth a visit, with its impressive lava rock formations and crystal-clear water.
- The town of Acireale is known for its beautiful baroque architecture, while nearby Catania is a bustling city with a vibrant nightlife and historic landmarks.

Tips for Visiting Mount Etna and the Northeast Coast

- It is important to dress appropriately for the weather and the terrain, as the climate on Mount Etna can be unpredictable and the hiking trails can be challenging.
- Visitors should be aware of the potential hazards associated with visiting an active volcano, such as lava flows, ash clouds, and gas emissions.
- It is recommended to book tours and activities in advance, as they can be popular and may fill up quickly during peak season.
- Visitors should also be respectful of the local environment and follow all safety guidelines and regulations.

Mount Etna and the Northeast Coast offer a unique and unforgettable experience for visitors to Sicily, with their stunning natural beauty, rich history, and diverse attractions.

With careful planning and preparation, visitors can enjoy all that this region has to offer while staying safe and respectful of the local environment.

Taormina and the Eastern Seaboard

Taormina is a picturesque hilltop town located on the east coast of Sicily, offering stunning views of the Mediterranean Sea and Mount Etna. The town is known for its charming medieval streets, ancient Greek theater, and luxurious resorts. Taormina has attracted visitors since the 18th century, when it became a popular destination for wealthy Europeans on the Grand Tour.

Taormina's history and culture

Taormina has a rich history dating back to ancient times, when it was founded by the Greeks in the 4th century BC. The town was later conquered by the Romans, who left their mark in the form of the impressive ruins of the Roman theater. Taormina also played a significant role in the Norman period and the Middle Ages, when it was a major center of commerce and culture.

Must-see attractions in Taormina

Ancient Greek Theater - The ancient Greek theater in Taormina is one of the town's most popular attractions, and for good reason. Built in the 3rd century BC, the theater is still used today for performances and concerts. The theater offers breathtaking views of the Mediterranean Sea and Mount Etna, making it an ideal spot for taking in the beauty of the region. Visitors can explore the theater on their own or take a guided tour.

Piazza del Duomo - Piazza del Duomo is the main square in Taormina, and it's a great place to start exploring the town. The square is surrounded by beautiful historic buildings, including the Cathedral of San Nicola, the Palazzo dei Duchi di Santo Stefano, and the Palazzo Corvaja. The square is a popular spot for locals and tourists alike, and it's a great place to relax and soak up the atmosphere.

Corso Umberto - Corso Umberto is Taormina's main street, and it's lined with charming shops, cafes, and restaurants. The street is a pedestrian-only zone, making it a great place for a leisurely stroll. Visitors can browse the many boutiques and shops selling everything from artisanal crafts to high-end fashion.

Villa Comunale - Villa Comunale is a stunning public garden located on the outskirts of Taormina. The garden offers breathtaking views of the Mediterranean Sea and Mount Etna, and it's a great place to relax and enjoy the beauty of the region. The garden is home to a variety of plants and trees, as well as a small pond and a historic villa.

Cathedral of San Nicola - The Cathedral of San Nicola is located in the heart of Taormina, and it's a great example of Sicilian Baroque architecture. The cathedral was built in the 13th century, and it's dedicated to Saint Nicholas of Bari. Visitors can admire the ornate interior of the cathedral, including its impressive frescoes and sculptures.

Excursions and day trips from Taormina

One of the great advantages of staying in Taormina is the variety of excursions and day trips available in the surrounding area. Here are a few suggestions for things to do and see outside of Taormina:

Mount Etna

Mount Etna is one of the most popular day trips from Taormina. This active volcano, located about an hour's drive from Taormina, is the highest in Europe and offers breathtaking views of the surrounding landscape. Visitors can take a cable car to the summit, explore the various hiking trails, or even take a guided tour of the volcano.

Isola Bella

Isola Bella, also known as the "Pearl of the Ionian Sea", is a tiny island located just off the coast of Taormina. This beautiful island is home to a nature reserve, a beach, and a charming baroque villa. Visitors can take a boat tour around the island, swim in the crystal-clear waters, or simply relax on the beach.

Noto and the Baroque towns

The Baroque towns of southeastern Sicily, including Noto, Ragusa, and Modica, are known for their stunning architecture and rich cultural heritage. Visitors can take a guided tour of these towns to learn about their history and see their beautiful churches, palaces, and public buildings.

Catania

Catania, located just a short drive from Taormina, is the second-largest city in Sicily and offers a wealth of cultural and historical attractions. Highlights include the Cathedral of Saint Agatha, the Roman Amphitheater, and the Ursino Castle. Visitors can also explore the bustling markets and sample the city's famous street food.

Castelmola

The charming hilltop town of Castelmola, located just a few kilometers from Taormina, offers stunning views of the Ionian Sea and the surrounding countryside. Visitors can explore the town's narrow streets, visit the ancient castle, and sample the local almond wine.

Recommendations for dining and shopping in Taormina

Taormina is known for its delicious Sicilian cuisine, and visitors can find a wide range of restaurants and cafes offering traditional dishes such as pasta alla Norma, caponata, and arancini. For shopping, visitors can explore the many boutiques and shops along Corso Umberto, offering everything from artisanal crafts to high-end fashion.

Taormina and the Eastern Seaboard offer visitors a unique blend of history, culture, and natural beauty. From the ancient Greek theater to the stunning views of Mount Etna, there is something for everyone in this beautiful corner of Sicily. Whether you're looking for relaxation, adventure, or culture, Taormina and the surrounding area will not disappoint.

Trapani and the West Coast

Trapani is a city located on the west coast of Sicily, known for its stunning beaches, ancient architecture, and excellent seafood. The city has a rich history and cultural heritage, and visitors will find plenty to see and do in Trapani and the surrounding area.

Trapani's history and culture

Trapani has a long and rich history, dating back to ancient times. The city was once a powerful trading center, and its strategic location on the Mediterranean made it a coveted prize for many conquerors over the centuries. Visitors to Trapani can explore the city's many historical and cultural landmarks, including the impressive Cathedral of San Lorenzo, the 17th-century Palazzo della Giudecca, and the Torre di Ligny, a medieval watchtower that offers breathtaking views of the coastline.

Must-see attractions in Trapani

Cathedral of San Lorenzo

The Cathedral of San Lorenzo is a stunning example of Baroque architecture and one of Trapani's most iconic landmarks. The cathedral was built in the 17th century on the site of an earlier church and features a beautiful marble facade, intricate carvings, and a soaring bell tower. Inside, visitors can admire the ornate altars and paintings, as well as the tombs of several local saints.

Fish Market

Trapani's bustling fish market is a must-visit for foodies and anyone interested in local culture. The market is located near the port and is a colorful, noisy hub of activity, with vendors selling a wide variety of fresh fish and seafood. Visitors can sample the catch of the day, watch the fishermen unload their boats, and soak up the lively atmosphere.

Palazzo della Giudecca

The Palazzo della Giudecca is a magnificent palace located in the heart of Trapani's historic center. The palace was built in the 17th century and features a grand facade decorated with intricate carvings and frescoes. Inside, visitors can explore the ornate halls and chambers, which are filled with antique furniture, paintings, and other treasures.

Torre di Ligny

The Torre di Ligny is a medieval watchtower that overlooks the sea and offers breathtaking views of the coastline. The tower was built in the 17th century as part of Trapani's defensive system and was used to warn the city of approaching ships. Today, the tower houses a museum that displays artifacts from Trapani's maritime history, as well as exhibitions on local culture and traditions.

Museum of Prehistoric and Ethnographic Art

The Museum of Prehistoric and Ethnographic Art is a fascinating museum that showcases the ancient cultures that once inhabited Sicily. The museum's collection includes artifacts from the Neolithic period, the Bronze Age, and the Greek and Roman eras, as well as objects from the local Arab and Norman cultures. Visitors can see pottery, jewelry, weapons, and other items that provide a glimpse into the region's rich history.

Church of Purgatorio

The Church of Purgatorio is a Baroque masterpiece located in the heart of Trapani's old town. The church is known for its impressive facade, which features a row of life-size statues depicting scenes from the Passion of Christ. Inside, visitors can admire the ornate altars and frescoes, as well as the famous Mysteries of Trapani, a series of sculptures that are carried through the streets during Holy Week.

Excursions and day trips from Trapani

Trapani is an excellent base for exploring the surrounding area, with many excursions and day trips available to visitors. Here are some of the top options:

Egadi Islands

The Egadi Islands are a group of three picturesque islands just off the coast of Trapani. Visitors can take a ferry from Trapani to the islands and spend the day exploring their many attractions. Favignana is the largest and most popular island, with beautiful beaches, crystal-clear waters, and a charming town center. Levanzo is the smallest of the three islands, with stunning cliffs and hidden coves perfect for snorkeling and swimming. Marettimo is the most remote and least visited, with rugged coastlines and excellent hiking trails.

Segesta and Selinunte

Segesta and Selinunte are two ancient Greek archaeological sites located just a short drive from

Trapani. Segesta features a well-preserved Doric temple, an impressive amphitheater, and stunning views of the surrounding countryside. Selinunte is a larger site, with several temples, a marketplace, and other impressive ruins. Both sites offer a fascinating glimpse into Sicily's rich history and cultural heritage.

Marsala

Marsala is a historic town located about 30 minutes from Trapani, known for its excellent wines and fascinating archaeological sites. Visitors can explore the town's many wineries and taste some of the famous Marsala wine, or visit the archaeological park, which features the remains of an ancient Phoenician city and a Roman amphitheater.

San Vito Lo Capo

San Vito Lo Capo is a beautiful seaside town located about an hour's drive from Trapani. The town is famous for its stunning beach, which is considered one of the best in Sicily. Visitors can also explore the town's many shops, restaurants, and bars, or take a boat tour along the coastline to see the area's many caves and coves.

Zingaro Nature Reserve

Zingaro Nature Reserve is a beautiful protected area located along the coast between Trapani and San Vito Lo Capo. The reserve features rugged cliffs, crystal-clear waters, and beautiful hiking trails, making it an ideal destination for nature lovers and outdoor enthusiasts. Visitors can explore the reserve on foot or by boat, and may encounter a variety of wildlife, including wild boars, foxes, and eagles.

Recommendations for dining and shopping in Trapani

Trapani is known for its excellent seafood, and visitors will find plenty of local restaurants serving fresh fish and shellfish. Some of the most popular dishes in the area include spaghetti con le sarde (spaghetti with sardines), busiate alla trapanese (pasta with pesto and tomatoes), and couscous alla trapanese (couscous with fish and vegetables). Visitors can also sample the local wines, including the sweet Marsala wine, which is produced in the nearby town of the same name.

For shopping, visitors can explore Trapani's many artisanal shops and boutiques, which sell handmade pottery, textiles, and other local crafts. The city's bustling markets are also a great place to find fresh produce, cheeses, and other regional specialties.

Trapani and the West Coast of Sicily offer visitors a fascinating blend of history, culture, and natural beauty. From the city's ancient landmarks and charming streets to the stunning beaches and picturesque hilltop towns, there is something for everyone in this part of Sicily.

The Aeolian Islands

The Aeolian Islands are a volcanic archipelago located off the northern coast of Sicily. The islands are named after Aeolus, the god of the winds, as they are known for their strong and unpredictable winds. The seven islands that make up the Aeolian Islands are Lipari, Vulcano, Salina, Stromboli, Panarea, Alicudi, and Filicudi. Each island has its own unique charm and character, offering visitors a chance to explore a variety of landscapes, from dramatic volcanic peaks to pristine beaches and crystal-clear waters.

History and culture of the Aeolian Islands

The Aeolian Islands have a rich history dating back to ancient times. The islands were first inhabited by the Greeks in the 4th century BC, and over the centuries they were ruled by various powers, including the Romans, the Byzantines, and the Normans. Today, the Aeolian Islands are a popular destination for tourists from around the world, offering a unique blend of natural beauty, cultural heritage, and modern amenities.

Must-see attractions on the Aeolian Islands

Each of the Aeolian Islands has its own unique attractions and activities. Here are some of the must-see sights on each island:

Lipari: The largest and most populous of the Aeolian Islands, Lipari is known for its historic town center, ancient Greek ruins, and beautiful beaches.

Vulcano: This island is home to one of the most active volcanoes in Europe, which can be climbed by visitors. Vulcano is also known for its therapeutic mud baths and hot springs.

Salina: This island is known for its lush vegetation, charming villages, and scenic hiking trails. Salina is also famous for its capers, which are grown on the island and used in many local dishes.

Stromboli: This island is dominated by a constantly active volcano, which can be seen spewing lava and ash into the air at night. Stromboli is also known for its black sand beaches and picturesque town center.

Panarea: This small and exclusive island is a favorite destination of the jet set, offering luxurious accommodations, high-end shopping, and world-class dining.

Alicudi: This remote and rugged island is the perfect destination for nature lovers and adventurers, with its rugged coastline, pristine waters, and stunning hiking trails.

Filicudi: This island is known for its rugged beauty and unspoiled natural landscapes, offering visitors a chance to experience the wild beauty of the Aeolian Islands.

Excursions and day trips from the Aeolian Islands

The Aeolian Islands are located close to several other popular destinations in Sicily, making them an ideal base for day trips and excursions. Some of the popular day trips from the Aeolian Islands include:

Taormina: This charming town on the eastern coast of Sicily is known for its ancient Greek theater, stunning views of Mount Etna, and picturesque old town.

Cefalù: This picturesque town on the northern coast of Sicily is famous for its medieval cathedral, beautiful beaches, and vibrant nightlife.

Catania: This bustling city on the eastern coast of Sicily is known for its rich history, vibrant street markets, and delicious street food.

Recommendations for dining and shopping on the Aeolian Islands

The Aeolian Islands are known for their delicious cuisine, which features fresh seafood, locally grown produce, and traditional Sicilian dishes. Some of the popular local specialties include caponata (a sweet and sour vegetable stew), pasta alla norma (pasta with eggplant and tomato sauce), and granita (a refreshing shaved ice dessert).

There are also plenty of opportunities for shopping on the Aeolian Islands, with many local shops and markets selling handmade crafts, ceramics, and souvenirs. Some of the top dining and shopping destinations on the Aeolian Islands include:

Lipari: Lipari is home to many excellent restaurants and shops, offering a variety of local specialties and souvenirs. Some popular restaurants include Ristorante Filippino and La Piazzeria, while popular shops include Ceramiche Stefania di Bernardo and Boutiques del Corso.

Vulcano: Vulcano is known for its delicious seafood restaurants and unique shopping opportunities, with many local artisans selling handmade crafts and souvenirs. Popular restaurants include Ristorante Eoliano and Ristorante Il Diavolo, while popular shops include Vibo Ceramica and Artigianato Vulcano.

Salina: Salina is famous for its delicious capers and local wine, making it a popular destination for foodies. Some popular restaurants include La Sirena and Mamma Santina, while popular shops include Il Posto delle Fragole and Il Girasole.

Stromboli: Stromboli is known for its high-end restaurants and exclusive boutiques, making it a favorite destination of the jet set. Some popular restaurants include Il Gabbiano and La Lampara, while popular shops include Le Trois Soeurs and Stromboli Blue.

Panarea: Panarea is known for its luxurious restaurants and high-end shopping, with many designer boutiques and upscale restaurants catering to the rich and famous. Popular restaurants include Da Pina and Hotel Raya, while popular shops include Antonio Marras and Dodo.

Alicudi: Alicudi is a remote island with few tourist amenities, making it the perfect destination for those looking for an off-the-beaten-path experience. There are a few local restaurants and shops on the island, offering a taste of traditional Aeolian culture.

Filicudi: Filicudi is known for its unspoiled natural landscapes and simple way of life, with few tourist amenities and a relaxed atmosphere. There are a few local restaurants and shops on the island, offering a taste of traditional Aeolian culture.

The Pelagie Islands

The Pelagie Islands are a group of three islands located south of Sicily in the Mediterranean Sea.

The islands are named Lampedusa, Linosa, and Lampione, with Lampedusa being the largest and most popular.

History and culture of the Pelagie Islands

The Pelagie Islands have a rich history dating back to ancient times, with evidence of Phoenician and Roman settlements on Lampedusa. The islands have also been influenced by Arab and Norman cultures, with a unique blend of traditions and customs. Today, the Pelagie Islands are known for their natural beauty and crystal-clear waters, making them a popular destination for diving, snorkeling, and beach-going.

Must-see attractions on the Pelagie Islands

Rabbit Beach: This stunning beach on Lampedusa Island is often ranked as one of the most beautiful beaches in the world. With crystal-clear turquoise waters and soft white sand, Rabbit Beach is a paradise for beach lovers. The beach is surrounded by cliffs and rock formations, making it a great spot for snorkeling and diving.

Cala Croce: Another beautiful beach on Lampedusa Island, Cala Croce is known for its stunning views and unique rock formations. The beach is surrounded by cliffs and caves, making it a popular spot for exploring.

Guitgia Lighthouse: Located on Lampedusa Island, the Guitgia Lighthouse is a historic landmark that offers panoramic views of the sea. The lighthouse was built in the 19th century and is still in operation today. Visitors can climb to the top for breathtaking views of the island and surrounding waters.

Linosa Island: Known for its volcanic landscape and rugged terrain, Linosa Island is a great spot for hiking and exploring. The island offers stunning views of the sea and surrounding islands, with hiking trails and natural pools to discover.

Marine Protected Area of Lampedusa: This protected area is home to diverse marine life and is a popular spot for snorkeling and diving. Visitors can swim with sea turtles, explore underwater caves, and spot colorful fish and coral.

Lampione Island: The smallest of the Pelagie Islands, Lampione is uninhabited and offers a rugged and pristine landscape. Visitors can explore the island's rocky terrain and spot a variety of wildlife, including sea birds and lizards.

Excursions and day trips from the Pelagie Islands

Visitors to the Pelagie Islands can take advantage of a variety of excursions and day trips to explore the surrounding area. Here are some popular options:

Boat tours: There are a number of boat tours available from Lampedusa and Linosa that allow visitors to explore the surrounding waters and nearby islands. Some tours include stops at nearby beaches or snorkeling spots, while others offer the chance to see marine life such as dolphins and sea turtles. Many tour operators offer both half-day and full-day options.

Scuba diving: The waters surrounding the Pelagie Islands are known for their clear visibility and diverse marine life, making them an excellent destination for scuba diving. There are a number of dive centers on Lampedusa and Linosa that offer equipment rental and guided dives for both beginners and experienced divers.

Tunisian day trips: The Pelagie Islands are located relatively close to the coast of Tunisia, and there are a number of day trips available for those who want to experience North African culture and history. Tunisian cities such as Sfax and Djerba can be visited in a day trip from Lampedusa, with tours typically including transportation, a guide, and some free time for exploring.

Hiking and nature walks: Both Lampedusa and Linosa offer opportunities for hiking and nature walks. Lampedusa's rugged landscape is home to several hiking trails, including a trail that leads to the Guitgia lighthouse. Linosa's volcanic landscape offers a unique and challenging terrain for hikers, with trails that lead to natural pools and scenic overlooks.

Cultural tours: For those interested in history and culture, there are a number of tours available that focus on the Pelagie Islands' unique heritage. These tours may include visits to historic sites such as the Roman ruins on Lampedusa or the Arab-Norman castle on Linosa.

Recommendations for dining and shopping on the Pelagie Islands

Recommendations for Dining on the Pelagie Islands

Seafood

One of the must-try dishes on the Pelagie Islands is fresh seafood. The islands' proximity to the sea means that fish and shellfish are often caught the same day they are served.

Some popular seafood dishes to try include spaghetti alle vongole (spaghetti with clams), pasta with swordfish, and grilled octopus.

A recommended restaurant for seafood is Il Veliero in Lampedusa, which offers a wide variety of seafood dishes and is known for its fresh ingredients and attentive service.

Local Specialties

- The Pelagie Islands have a unique culinary heritage, with a blend of Italian, Arab, and North African influences.
- One local specialty to try is couscous, which is traditionally made with fish and served with a spicy tomato sauce. Another is panelle, a fried chickpea fritter that is a popular street food in Sicily.
- For a taste of local cuisine, La Piazzetta in Lampedusa is a recommended restaurant that offers a variety of traditional dishes made with locally sourced ingredients.

Recommendations for Shopping on the Pelagie Islands

Handcrafted Items

- The Pelagie Islands are known for their traditional handicrafts, including jewelry, ceramics, and woven textiles.

- One recommended shop to visit is Arancio in Lampedusa, which offers a wide variety of locally made jewelry and crafts.
- Another shop to check out is Casa del Mare in Linosa, which sells a variety of handcrafted items such as woven baskets and embroidered linens.

Local Food Products

- Visitors to the Pelagie Islands can also find a variety of locally made food products to take home as souvenirs or gifts.
- One popular item is bottarga, a cured fish roe that is often grated over pasta or used as a seasoning.
- Other local products to try include olive oil, honey, and almond-based sweets.
- A recommended shop for food products is La Bottega del Gusto in Lampedusa, which specializes in local products made with high-quality ingredients.

Overall, the Pelagie Islands offer a unique and breathtaking destination for travelers looking to explore the natural beauty and rich history of southern Italy.

Chapter 4: Discovering Sicily's Hidden Gems

The Baroque Towns of the Southeast

The Baroque style became the dominant style of Sicilian architecture in the 17th and 18th centuries and is characterized by its ornate details, dramatic curves, and extravagant decoration. This style was embraced by Sicily's aristocracy and the Catholic Church, who used it to express their wealth, power, and religious devotion.

Today, the towns of Noto, Modica, Ragusa, and Scicli are some of the most beautiful examples of Sicilian Baroque architecture. These towns were almost completely destroyed by the devastating earthquake of 1693, but were rebuilt in the Baroque style, resulting in a uniformity of architecture that is truly unique.

Here's a closer look at each of these towns:

Noto: Known as the "capital of Baroque," Noto is often referred to as an "open-air museum" due to its many stunning examples of Baroque architecture. The town's central avenue, Corso Vittorio Emanuele, is lined with impressive palaces, churches, and other public buildings that showcase the beauty of the Baroque style.

Modica: This town is famous for its chocolate, which is made using traditional methods and has a unique flavor due to the use of ground cocoa beans. Modica is also renowned for its many Baroque churches and palaces, including the Church of San Giorgio and the Palazzo Polara.

Ragusa: This town is split into two parts: Ragusa Superiore, the modern upper town, and Ragusa Ibla, the historic lower town. Both areas are known for their Baroque architecture, with Ragusa Ibla being home to many of the town's most beautiful buildings. Highlights include the Cathedral of San Giorgio and the Palazzo Zacco.

Scicli: This small town is often overlooked by tourists but is a true hidden gem of Sicilian Baroque architecture. The town's narrow streets and steep staircases are lined with ornate facades, and the Church of San Matteo is a must-see attraction.

Visitors to the Baroque towns of the southeast can take guided tours, explore on foot, or simply wander and discover the architectural treasures that lie around every corner. In addition to the Baroque architecture, visitors can also enjoy local food, markets, and festivals that celebrate the unique culture and traditions of Sicily. The southeast of Sicily is a region that is full of surprises and delights, and the Baroque towns are just one of the many reasons to visit this beautiful island.

The Roman Villa of Piazza Armerina

The Roman Villa of Piazza Armerina is one of the most impressive examples of Roman architecture and art in Sicily. Located in the heart of the island, it was built in the 4th century AD and rediscovered in the late 19th century. Today, it is a UNESCO World Heritage Site and a popular attraction for visitors to Sicily.

The villa covers an area of about 14,000 square meters and is believed to have been the country residence of a wealthy Roman family. The villa is famous for its exceptional mosaic floors, which cover almost every room and depict a wide range of subjects, from mythological scenes to hunting and fishing scenes, and even intricate geometric patterns.

Some of the most famous mosaics in the villa include the "Bikini Girls," a series of female athletes depicted wearing only a small piece of fabric around their waists, and the "Great Hunt," a large mosaic that shows a hunting scene with dozens of animals and hunters.

In addition to the mosaics, the villa also features an extensive collection of Roman artifacts, including statues, sculptures, and other decorative elements. Visitors can take a guided tour of the site or explore it on their own with an audio guide.

The villa is open year-round, although hours may vary depending on the season. It is recommended to book tickets in advance, especially during the peak tourist season in the summer months. Visitors should plan to spend at least a few hours at the villa to fully appreciate its beauty and history.

The Roman Villa of Piazza Armerina is also known for its well-preserved architecture. The villa is divided into three main sections: the residential area, the service area, and the thermal baths. The residential area includes a series of rooms, each with its own mosaic floor, that were likely used for dining, sleeping, and entertaining guests. The service area contains rooms for servants and storage, while the thermal baths feature a series of rooms for bathing and relaxation.

In addition to its impressive art and architecture, the Roman Villa of Piazza Armerina is also significant for what it tells us about daily life in ancient Rome. The mosaics, for example, offer a glimpse into the pastimes and interests of the villa's inhabitants, while the artifacts provide insights into the technology, craftsmanship, and trade of the time.

To fully appreciate the Roman Villa of Piazza Armerina, visitors should take the time to explore the site in detail, paying close attention to the intricate details of the mosaics and the architecture. A guided tour can provide valuable context and background information, while an audio guide can allow visitors to explore at their own pace.

Overall, the Roman Villa of Piazza Armerina is a must-see attraction for anyone interested in history, art, or architecture. Its stunning mosaics, impressive architecture, and fascinating history make it one of the most important and memorable sites in Sicily.

The Salt Pans of Trapani

The Salt Pans of Trapani are an important part of Sicilian history and culture. Salt production has been a major industry in Sicily for centuries, and the salt pans in Trapani and Paceco are still active today. The process of producing salt is fascinating and worth learning about during your travels in Sicily.

The salt pans in Trapani and Paceco are a series of shallow ponds that are filled with sea water. The water is allowed to evaporate, leaving behind the salt. The salt is then harvested by hand and piled into large mounds, where it dries in the sun. The salt is then cleaned, sorted, and packaged for distribution.

The salt pans of Trapani are not only important for their salt production, but also for the unique ecosystem that they create. The salt pans are home to many species of birds, including flamingos, which can be seen wading through the shallow water. The salt pans also provide a habitat for many species of plants and animals that are adapted to the saline environment.

In addition to the salt pans themselves, there are many other interesting things to see and do in the area. The Salt Museum in Nubia provides a detailed history of salt production in Sicily and is a great place to learn about the process. The nearby town of Marsala is also worth a visit, as it is famous for its dessert wine and has a beautiful historic center.

If you're lucky enough to be in Trapani during the summer, you might be able to experience the Salt Festival. This annual festival celebrates the history and culture of salt production in the area and includes music, dancing, and of course, plenty of salt.

Visiting the salt pans of Trapani is a great way to experience the natural beauty and rich history of Sicily. There are several ways to explore the area, including guided tours and self-guided walks. If you're interested in learning more about the salt production process, it's recommended to join a guided tour to get a more in-depth look at how the salt is harvested and processed.

One of the best ways to explore the salt pans is by foot or bicycle. There are several trails that wind through the salt pans, providing visitors with stunning views of the surrounding landscape and wildlife. The salt pans are also a popular spot for birdwatching, as they are home to many species of birds, including flamingos, herons, and egrets.

If you're interested in learning more about the history and culture of the area, be sure to visit the

Salt Museum in Nubia. The museum provides a detailed look at the salt production process, as well as the cultural and economic impact of salt on the region.

Finally, no visit to the salt pans of Trapani would be complete without trying some of the locally-produced salt. The salt from Trapani is known for its high quality and unique flavor, thanks to the area's unique climate and salt production methods. You can purchase salt at the Salt Museum or at local shops and markets throughout the region.

Overall, a visit to the salt pans of Trapani is a must-see attraction for anyone interested in the history, culture, and natural beauty of Sicily. Be sure to add it to your itinerary when planning your trip to Sicily.

The Nature Reserves of Sicily

Sicily is not just a land of history and culture, it's also a land of stunning natural beauty. The island has several nature reserves that offer visitors the chance to explore the island's diverse landscapes and ecosystems. Here are a few nature reserves that are worth visiting:

Zingaro Nature Reserve: Located on the northwest coast of Sicily, Zingaro Nature Reserve is a protected area that boasts some of the island's most breathtaking views. The reserve is home to a variety of flora and fauna, including over 40 species of birds and the rare Corsican red deer. Visitors can hike along the reserve's trails, which wind through rocky cliffs and along turquoise waters.

Vendicari Nature Reserve: Situated on the southeast coast of Sicily, Vendicari Nature Reserve is a protected wetland area that serves as a stopover point for migratory birds. Visitors to the reserve can observe a variety of bird species, including flamingos, herons, and storks. The reserve is also home to sandy beaches and ancient ruins, including a Byzantine necropolis.

Nebrodi Nature Reserve: Located in the northeast part of the island, Nebrodi Nature Reserve is a vast forested area that spans over 86,000 hectares. The reserve is home to a variety of wildlife, including wild boar, roe deer, and golden eagles. Visitors can explore the reserve's hiking trails, which offer stunning views of the surrounding mountains and valleys.

Madonie Nature Park: Located in the north-central part of the island, Madonie Nature Park is a protected area that spans over 40,000 hectares. The park is home to a variety of flora and fauna, including the Madonie fir tree and the Sicilian shrew. Visitors can hike along the park's trails, which lead to ancient hilltop towns and stunning vistas.

These nature reserves offer a glimpse into the diverse ecosystems and natural beauty of Sicily. Visitors who are interested in nature and hiking will find these reserves to be a welcome break from the hustle and bustle of the island's cities and tourist attractions.

In addition to the nature reserves mentioned above, there are several other natural attractions worth exploring in Sicily. Mount Etna, the largest active volcano in Europe, is a popular destination for visitors who want to witness the power and beauty of nature. The volcano is located on the east coast of

Sicily and can be reached by car or bus. Visitors can take a cable car and then a jeep to reach the summit, where they can enjoy stunning views of the surrounding landscape.

Sicily's beaches are also a major draw for visitors who want to soak up the sun and enjoy the Mediterranean Sea. Some of the most popular beaches in Sicily include San Vito lo Capo, Mondello, and Isola Bella. These beaches offer crystal-clear waters, soft sand, and stunning views of the coastline.

Finally, Sicily is home to several beautiful parks and gardens that are perfect for a leisurely stroll or picnic. The Villa Bellini, located in the heart of Catania, is a beautiful park that features fountains, statues, and botanical gardens. The Orto Botanico di Palermo is a historic botanical garden that is home to over 12,000 species of plants. The gardens offer a peaceful respite from the city and are a great place to relax and enjoy the beauty of nature.

In conclusion, Sicily's nature reserves, beaches, parks, and gardens offer visitors a chance to connect with the island's natural beauty and diversity.

Exploring these hidden gems can be a welcome break from the crowds and tourist attractions, and a chance to experience the island in a more authentic and meaningful way.

The Wine Country of the West

The importance of wine in Sicilian culture cannot be overstated. With a rich history of wine production dating back thousands of years, Sicily is home to many notable wine regions, each with its own unique grape varietals and winemaking traditions.

Located in the western part of the island, the wine country of Sicily is characterized by rolling hills and fertile valleys that provide the ideal growing conditions for grapes. Here are some of the top wine regions to explore:

Marsala: Located on the western coast of Sicily, Marsala is perhaps the most famous wine region on the island. This region is known for its sweet dessert wines, which are made using a unique process that involves fortifying the wine with brandy. A visit to

Marsala should include a stop at one of the many wineries that offer tastings and tours.

Alcamo: Located in the northwestern part of Sicily, Alcamo is a small town that is home to some excellent wineries. The wines of this region are made primarily from the Catarratto grape, which is known for producing crisp, refreshing white wines. Some of the top wineries to visit in Alcamo include Cantine Europa and Fazio Wines.

Castelvetrano: Located in the southwestern part of the island, Castelvetrano is known for its olive oil production as well as its wine. The wines of this region are made from a variety of grape varietals, including Nero d'Avola and Grillo. A visit to Castelvetrano should include a stop at the Planeta Winery, which is one of the top producers in the area.

In addition to visiting wineries and sampling the local wines, visitors to the wine country of the west can also explore the beautiful countryside and enjoy the local cuisine. Many of the wineries offer guided tours that include wine tastings as well as traditional Sicilian meals, such as pasta with fresh tomato sauce and grilled fish.

Some other notable wine regions in the western part of Sicily include the Belice Valley, Trapani, and Pantelleria. The Belice Valley, located in the southwestern part of the island, is known for its Nero d'Avola and Perricone grape varietals. Trapani, located in the northwest part of Sicily, is known for its Zibibbo grape varietal, which is used to produce sweet wines as well as dry whites. Pantelleria, a small island off the coast of Sicily, is known for its sweet Moscato di Pantelleria wine, which is made from the Muscat of Alexandria grape.

When visiting the wine country of the west, it is also worth exploring some of the other culinary traditions of the region. Sicilian cuisine is characterized by its use of fresh, locally sourced ingredients, and many of the dishes feature seafood, pasta, and olive oil. Some of the must-try dishes include pasta con le sarde (pasta with sardines), caponata (a vegetable stew), and arancini (fried rice balls).

Overall, the wine country of the west offers visitors a unique and unforgettable experience. From the rolling hills and scenic vineyards to the delicious food and wine, this region is a true gem of Sicily. Whether you are a wine enthusiast or simply looking to experience the beauty and culture of Sicily, a visit to the wine country of the west should be on your itinerary.

Chapter 5: Culinary Delights

Sicilian cuisine is one of the most popular and unique cuisines in Italy, characterized by a blend of cultures and flavors. Sicily, the largest island in the Mediterranean Sea, has been a melting pot of civilizations and cultures throughout history, including the Phoenicians, Greeks, Romans, Arabs, Normans, and Spanish, each contributing to its rich culinary heritage.

Sicilian cuisine is characterized by its simplicity, fresh ingredients, and bold flavors. The island's fertile land and warm climate provide an abundance of fresh produce, including citrus fruits, olives, tomatoes, eggplants, and peppers, which are used extensively in its cuisine. Seafood is also a staple in Sicilian cuisine, owing to its location along the Mediterranean coast.

The island's cuisine is renowned for its pasta dishes, including spaghetti with clams, pasta alla Norma, and pasta con le sarde, which are prepared with fresh herbs, vegetables, and seafood. Another popular dish is arancini, fried rice balls filled with meat, cheese, or vegetables. Sicilian cuisine is also known for its sweets, including cannoli, cassata, and granita.

Sicily is also famous for its food festivals and markets, where locals and visitors can taste traditional Sicilian dishes, street food, and local wines. One of the most famous markets in Sicily is Vucciria Market, located in the heart of Palermo, where you can find a wide range of fresh produce, meats, fish, and street food.

Sicilian cuisine is not complete without its wines, which are renowned for their unique flavors and aromas. Nero d'Avola, the most popular red wine in Sicily, pairs perfectly with meat and pasta dishes, while Marsala, a fortified wine from western Sicily, is perfect with cheese and desserts. Grillo, a crisp and fresh white wine, is the ideal pairing for seafood and salads.

In this chapter, we will explore the traditional Sicilian dishes and recipes, food festivals and markets, and wine and food pairings in Sicilian cuisine. We will also provide recommendations for the best Sicilian restaurants and street food spots to visit during your travels to Sicily. Get ready to indulge in the flavors of Sicily and experience the island's culinary delights like a local.

Traditional Sicilian Dishes and Recipes

Sicilian cuisine is a fusion of culinary traditions from Italy, Greece, Spain, and North Africa. From pasta dishes to seafood delicacies, Sicilian cuisine is known for its fresh ingredients, bold flavors, and unique combinations. Here are some of the most popular traditional Sicilian dishes and recipes that you must try during your visit to the island:

Pasta alla Norma: Eggplant and Tomato Sauce with Ricotta Cheese

Pasta alla Norma is a classic Sicilian pasta dish made with fried eggplant, tomato sauce, basil, and ricotta cheese. The dish is named after Vincenzo Bellini's opera "Norma," which was set in Sicily. The eggplant is sliced and fried until golden brown, then simmered in a rich tomato sauce with garlic, onions, and herbs. The pasta is then mixed with the eggplant and tomato sauce, and topped with crumbled ricotta cheese. Pasta alla Norma is a vegetarian-friendly dish that is hearty, flavorful, and easy to make.

Arancini: Fried Rice Balls with Meat, Cheese, or Vegetable Filling

Arancini are crispy and golden brown fried rice balls that are typically filled with ragù (meat sauce), mozzarella cheese, and peas. The rice is cooked with saffron and mixed with parmesan cheese, then formed into balls and filled with the ragù, cheese, and peas. The balls are then coated in breadcrumbs and deep-fried until crispy. Arancini are a popular street food snack in Sicily, and they can also be found in many Italian restaurants around the world.

Caponata: Eggplant and Vegetable Stew in Sweet and Sour Sauce

Caponata is a sweet and sour stew made with eggplant, tomatoes, capers, olives, and onions. The eggplant is sautéed until tender, then combined with the other ingredients and simmered in a sweet and sour sauce made with vinegar, sugar, and red pepper flakes. Caponata can be served hot or cold as a side dish, salad, or appetizer. It is a great vegetarian option that showcases the flavors of Sicilian cuisine.

Cassata: Ricotta and Sponge Cake with Candied Fruit and Chocolate

Cassata is a decadent dessert made with ricotta cheese, sponge cake, candied fruit, and chocolate. The sponge cake is soaked in liquor and layered with sweetened ricotta cheese, then covered in a layer of marzipan and decorated with candied fruit and chocolate shavings. Cassata is a traditional dessert that is often served during Easter and other festive occasions.

Granita: Shaved Ice with Fruit Syrup and Brioche

Granita is a refreshing and fruity dessert made with shaved ice and fruit syrup. The ice is shaved into a fine snow-like texture and mixed with syrup made from local fruits such as lemons, oranges, and strawberries. Granita is typically served with a soft and fluffy brioche bun, which is perfect for soaking up the syrup. Granita is a popular Sicilian treat that is perfect for a hot summer day.

Pasta con le Sarde: Pasta with Sardines, Fennel, and Pine Nuts

Pasta con le Sarde is a popular Sicilian pasta dish made with fresh sardines, wild fennel, and pine nuts. The dish is flavored with saffron, raisins, garlic, and onions, and is often served with bucatini or spaghetti. The sardines are cooked in a tomato-based sauce with fennel, raisins, and pine nuts, creating a unique blend of flavors that is both sweet and savory. This dish is a perfect representation of the mix of different culinary influences in Sicilian cuisine.

Involtini di Pesce Spada: Swordfish Roll-Ups with Bread Crumbs, Pine Nuts, and Raisins

Involtini di Pesce Spada is a delicious Sicilian seafood dish made with swordfish fillets rolled up with bread crumbs, pine nuts, and raisins. The rolls are then cooked in a tomato-based sauce with onions, garlic, and white wine, creating a flavorful and aromatic dish. This dish is a great example of how Sicilian cuisine uses sweet and savory flavors together to create unique dishes.

Cannoli: Fried Pastry Tubes filled with Sweet Ricotta Cream

Cannoli is a Sicilian dessert made of fried pastry tubes filled with sweet ricotta cream. The pastry dough is rolled out thin and cut into circles, then wrapped around metal tubes and deep-fried until golden brown. The tubes are then filled with a sweet ricotta cream flavored with vanilla, cinnamon, and orange zest. Cannoli is often garnished with chopped pistachios, candied fruit, or chocolate chips. This dessert is a must-try when visiting Sicily, as it is one of the most iconic and beloved desserts in Italian cuisine.

Gelato: Italian-Style Ice Cream in a Variety of Flavors

Gelato is the Italian version of ice cream, and Sicily is known for its delicious and creamy gelato. Gelato is made with fresh milk, cream, and sugar, and comes in a variety of flavors such as pistachio, hazelnut, chocolate, and fruit flavors like lemon and strawberry. Gelato is a perfect treat on a hot summer day and can be found in many gelato shops throughout the island.

Panelle: Fried Chickpea Fritters

Panelle is a popular Sicilian street food made with chickpea flour, water, and seasonings. The batter is fried until golden brown and crispy, then cut into strips and served as a snack or appetizer. Panelle is often served with bread or in a sandwich, making it a popular food item in Sicily. This dish is a great example of how simple ingredients can be transformed into a delicious and flavorful snack.

Sicilian cuisine is rich in history, culture, and flavors. From the iconic pasta alla Norma to the sweet and decadent cassata, Sicilian cuisine has something for everyone. Make sure to try these traditional dishes and recipes during your visit to Sicily, and don't forget to explore the local markets and food festivals to fully immerse yourself in the island's culinary delights.

Food Festivals and Markets in Sicily

Sicily is famous for its delicious cuisine, which is influenced by Mediterranean and Arab cultures. The island is home to many vibrant food festivals and markets that offer a unique opportunity to experience the local food and culture. Here are some of the best food festivals and markets to explore in Sicily:

Festa del Santissimo Salvatore

The Festa del Santissimo Salvatore is an annual festival that takes place in the historic city of Palermo. The festival is held to honor the patron saint of Palermo, and it's celebrated with street food, parades, and fireworks. The festival usually takes place in July, and it's a great opportunity to try some of the best street food in Sicily, including arancini, panelle, and sfincione.

Vucciria Market

The Vucciria Market is one of the most famous markets in Sicily, located in the historic district of Palermo. The market is a bustling hub of activity, with vendors selling fresh produce, seafood, meat, and local specialties like caponata and cannoli. The market is open daily except for Sundays and is a great place to sample the local food and immerse yourself in the vibrant culture of Palermo.

La Passeggiata

La Passeggiata is an evening stroll that takes place in many towns and cities in Sicily. During La Passeggiata, locals take a leisurely stroll through the streets, stopping at various food vendors and restaurants to sample the local specialties. The stroll usually takes place in the late afternoon or early evening and is a great way to experience the local food and culture.

Infiorata di Noto

The Infiorata di Noto is a festival that takes place in the town of Noto, located in southeastern Sicily. The festival is held in May and is a celebration of flowers and traditional Sicilian food. During the festival, the streets of Noto are decorated with elaborate floral arrangements, and local vendors sell traditional Sicilian food like arancini, cannoli, and granita.

Sagra del Pesce

The Sagra del Pesce is an annual fish festival that takes place in the coastal town of Aci Trezza, located on the eastern coast of Sicily. The festival is held in June and celebrates the town's fishing heritage. During the festival, local fishermen cook up fresh seafood dishes, including grilled fish, fried squid, and seafood pasta. The festival also features live music, dancing, and fireworks.

Mercato del Capo

The Mercato del Capo is a bustling market located in the heart of Palermo. The market is known for its fresh produce, meat, fish, and local specialties like pane ca meusa, a sandwich made with spleen and lung meat. The market is open daily except for Sundays and is a great place to experience the local food and culture.

Festival del Gelato Artigianale

The Festival del Gelato Artigianale is a festival celebrating Sicily's delicious gelato. The festival takes place in the town of Cefalù, located on the northern coast of Sicily, in July. During the festival, local gelato makers showcase their creations, and visitors can sample a wide variety of flavors, including traditional Sicilian flavors like pistachio and almond.

Festa di San Calogero

The Festa di San Calogero is an annual festival that takes place in the town of Agrigento, located on the southern coast of Sicily. The festival is held in July and celebrates the town's patron saint, San Calogero. During the festival, local vendors sell traditional Sicilian food, including pasta alla norma, caponata, and cannoli. The festival also features live music, dancing, and fireworks.

Sicily's food festivals and markets are a great way to experience the island's delicious cuisine and vibrant culture. From the fresh seafood at the Sagra del Pesce to the gelato at the Festival del Gelato Artigianale, there's something for every food lover in Sicily. So be sure to add some of these food festivals and markets to your itinerary when you visit the island.

Wine and Food Pairings in Sicilian Cuisine

Sicily is known for its diverse culinary scene that draws influences from different cultures and traditions. The island is home to a wide variety of wines that complement the flavors of the local cuisine. Here are some of the most popular wine and food pairings in Sicilian cuisine:

Nero d'Avola

Nero d'Avola is the most famous Sicilian red wine, known for its bold and fruity flavor. It pairs well with meat dishes such as grilled lamb, roasted beef, and braised pork. The wine's robustness can also stand up to the tomato-based sauces in Sicilian pasta dishes like spaghetti alla Norma or pasta con le sarde.

Marsala

Marsala is a fortified wine that originated from the town of Marsala in western Sicily. It comes in a range of styles, from dry to sweet, and is known for its nutty, caramel-like flavor. Marsala pairs well with aged cheeses, like Pecorino or Parmigiano-Reggiano, and is often used in cooking savory dishes like veal or chicken Marsala. Sweet Marsala is also commonly used in desserts such as tiramisu or zabaglione.

Grillo

Grillo is a crisp and refreshing white wine that is native to Sicily. It has citrus and tropical fruit notes that complement seafood dishes like grilled prawns, fried calamari, and seafood risotto. Grillo also pairs well with fresh salads and light pasta dishes.

Cannoli and Zibibbo

Cannoli is a Sicilian pastry filled with sweet ricotta cheese, candied fruit, and chocolate chips. Zibibbo is a sweet wine made from sun-dried grapes. Together, they create a perfect sweet and fruity pairing that is ideal for dessert. The wine's sweetness balances out the richness of the pastry, while its fruit notes complement the flavors of the filling.

Tips for Exploring Sicilian Wines and Cuisine

- Visit local wineries and vineyards to learn about the wine-making process and taste different varietals.
- Take a foodie tour or cooking class to discover the secrets of traditional Sicilian dishes and ingredients.
- Check out the menus of local restaurants and street food vendors to sample the best of Sicilian cuisine and wine pairings.
- Attend food and wine festivals throughout the year to taste the best of what Sicily has to offer.

Some additional tips for exploring Sicilian wines and cuisine:

Visit wine bars and enotecas (wine shops) to sample a variety of Sicilian wines. Many wine bars offer tasting flights or small pours, which allow you to try several wines without committing to a full glass or bottle. Enotecas often have a wide selection of local wines for sale, as well as knowledgeable staff who can offer recommendations based on your tastes and preferences.

Look for restaurants that specialize in Sicilian cuisine and have extensive wine lists featuring local varietals. Some restaurants also offer wine pairing menus, which provide a selection of wines to accompany each course of your meal.

Attend a wine or food festival in Sicily to experience the best of the island's cuisine and wine culture. Some of the most popular festivals include the Targa Florio wine festival in Palermo, the Vini di Vignaioli wine festival in Noto, and the Gusto Sicily food festival in Catania.

Take a cooking class to learn how to prepare traditional Sicilian dishes and discover the ingredients that make the cuisine so unique. Many cooking classes include a visit to a local market or farm to shop for ingredients, giving you a chance to see how locals shop and interact with the ingredients that make their cuisine so special.

Consider taking a guided food or wine tour to explore the island's culinary highlights with an expert guide. Some tours focus on a specific region or type of cuisine, while others offer a broader overview of Sicilian food and wine culture. A knowledgeable guide can help you navigate the menus, learn about the history and culture behind each dish, and discover hidden gems that you might otherwise miss.

The best Sicilian restaurants and street food spots to visit during your travels to Sicily

Sicily is a beautiful island in the Mediterranean Sea that is known for its stunning landscapes, rich history, and delicious food. The island's cuisine is influenced by a range of cultures, including Greek, Arab, and Spanish, resulting in a diverse range of flavors and dishes that are sure to tantalize your taste buds.

If you are planning to travel to Sicily and are looking for the best restaurants and street food spots to visit, here are some recommendations to help you enjoy the island's culinary delights:

Trattoria da Enzo is a must-visit restaurant in Taormina, a charming town on the east coast of the island. This family-owned eatery has been serving up traditional Sicilian cuisine for over 40 years. The menu includes dishes like pasta alla Norma, a pasta dish made with tomato sauce, eggplant, and ricotta salata, and arancini, fried rice balls filled with meat or cheese. Their homemade desserts, such as cannoli and cassata, are also worth trying.

Palermo is the largest city in Sicily and home to Antica Focacceria San Francesco, a historic street food spot that has been around since 1834. The menu includes classic Sicilian street food like panelle, chickpea fritters, and crocchè, potato croquettes. Sfincione, a type of Sicilian pizza, is another popular dish. The restaurant also has a sit-down area where you can enjoy your food in a relaxed atmosphere.

If you're in the mood for seafood, Osteria Nero d'Avola in Syracuse is a great choice. This cozy restaurant specializes in fish and seafood dishes, such as spaghetti alle vongole, pasta with clams, and fritto misto di mare, mixed fried seafood. Their pesce spada alla ghiotta, swordfish stewed with tomatoes, olives, and capers, is another popular dish.

For sweet treats, head to Pasticceria Maria Grammatico in Erice. This bakery has been making traditional Sicilian pastries and sweets for over 50 years. Their cassata, a cake made with sponge cake, ricotta cheese, and marzipan, is a must-try, as is their frutta martorana, marzipan fruit-shaped sweets. They also serve cannoli, Sicily's most famous pastry.

The Mercato del Capo in Palermo is a bustling market where you can sample a range of Sicilian street food. The pane con panelle, a sandwich made with chickpea fritters, is a must-try, as are the arancine, rice balls filled with meat or cheese. The market is also a great place to pick up fresh produce and local specialties like capers and olives.

La Madia in Licata is a Michelin-starred restaurant that offers a modern take on Sicilian cuisine. The chef, Pino Cuttaia, uses fresh, locally sourced ingredients to create innovative dishes like risotto with red shrimp, pistachio and sea urchin, and beef tenderloin with capers and caramelized onions.

Caffe Sicilia in Noto is an iconic cafe that serves some of the best gelato on the island. Their granita, a refreshing, slushy-like dessert made with fruit and ice, is also a must-try. The cafe's pastries and desserts are also popular, especially the cassatelle, a pastry filled with ricotta cheese, cinnamon, and chocolate.

Finally, Pizzeria La Pecora Nera in Catania is a casual pizzeria that serves delicious wood-fired pizzas. Their Diavola, with spicy salami, and Capricciosa, with ham, mushrooms, olives, and artichokes, are both popular choices.

In conclusion, Sicily is a food lover's paradise, with a wide range of restaurants and street food spots to satisfy all palates. Whether you're looking for traditional Sicilian dishes or innovative creations, there's something for everyone in this region. So, when you travel to Sicily, make sure to add some of these fantastic food spots to your itinerary:

- Trattoria da Enzo, Taormina - for traditional Sicilian cuisine, including pasta alla Norma and arancini.

- Antica Focacceria San Francesco, Palermo - for classic Sicilian street food like panelle, crocchè, and sfincione.

- Osteria Nero d'Avola, Syracuse - for delicious seafood dishes like spaghetti alle vongole and pesce spada alla ghiotta.

- Pasticceria Maria Grammatico, Erice - for traditional Sicilian sweets like cassata, frutta martorana, and cannoli.

- Mercato del Capo, Palermo - for a range of Sicilian street food, fresh produce, and local specialties like capers and olives.

- La Madia, Licata - for a modern take on Sicilian cuisine, with dishes like risotto with red shrimp and pistachio.

- Caffe Sicilia, Noto - for some of the best gelato, granita, and pastries on the island.

- Pizzeria La Pecora Nera, Catania - for delicious wood-fired pizzas, including the popular Diavola and Capricciosa.

In addition to these fantastic food spots, there are many other great restaurants and street food vendors to explore in Sicily. Some other traditional Sicilian dishes to try include pasta con le sarde (pasta with sardines), caponata (a vegetable dish made with eggplant, celery, and olives), and cannoli di ricotta (cannoli filled with sweet ricotta cheese). And, of course, don't forget to sample some of Sicily's delicious wines, like Nero d'Avola and Marsala.

Overall, Sicily is a food lover's paradise, with an incredible variety of flavors, ingredients, and culinary traditions. Whether you're a fan of traditional Sicilian dishes or innovative, modern cuisine, you're sure to find something to delight your taste buds in this stunning region of Italy.

Chapter 6: Practical Information and Tips

Getting to Sicily: Transportation and Travel Planning

Airports and Flights to Sicily:

Sicily has several airports with international and domestic flights. The largest airport is Catania–Fontanarossa Airport, followed by Palermo Airport, Trapani Airport, and Comiso Airport. Airlines such as Alitalia, Ryanair, EasyJet, and Vueling operate flights to Sicily from major cities in Europe and other parts of the world. Flight times can range from 1 to 5 hours depending on the departure point. It's advisable to book flights well in advance to secure better deals and availability.

Ferry Services to Sicily:

Ferries are an alternative mode of transportation to Sicily. The most popular routes are from the mainland Italian ports of Naples, Salerno, Civitavecchia, and Genoa. You can also take ferries from other Mediterranean ports such as Malta, Tunisia, and Sardinia. There are several ferry companies that operate to Sicily, including Grimaldi Lines, Tirrenia, and SNAV. Prices and schedules can vary depending on the season, so it's best to book in advance.

Train and Bus Services in Sicily:

Sicily has an extensive train and bus network, with connections to most major cities and towns on the island. Trenitalia operates the train services, while the bus services are operated by several companies such as AST, SAIS, and Interbus. The train journey from Palermo to Catania takes around 3 hours, while the bus journey can take up to 5 hours depending on the route. Tickets can be bought online, at train stations, or at bus terminals.

Car Rental and Driving in Sicily:

Renting a car is a popular option for tourists in Sicily, as it provides flexibility and convenience when exploring the island. There are several car rental companies that operate in Sicily, such as Hertz, Avis, and Europcar. Driving in Sicily can be challenging, especially in cities, as the roads can be narrow and chaotic. It's important to have a valid driver's license and insurance, and to be aware of the local driving regulations and parking restrictions.

Planning Your Itinerary:

When planning your itinerary to Sicily, it's important to consider the best times to visit, the weather, and any seasonal events that may affect your travel plans. The peak tourist season in Sicily is from June to September, when the weather is warm and sunny, and most attractions and beaches are open. However, this is also the busiest and most expensive time to travel. The shoulder seasons of April to May and October to November can offer pleasant weather, fewer crowds, and lower prices. Winter in Sicily can be rainy and chilly, but there are still some attractions and activities that can be enjoyed.

Travel Documents and Requirements:

When traveling to Sicily, it's important to have the necessary travel documents and requirements in order. Visitors from the European Union, the United States, Canada, and Australia do not need a visa for stays up to 90 days. However, a valid passport is required for all travelers. It's also recommended to have travel insurance that covers medical expenses, trip cancellation, and other unforeseen events.

Accommodation Options: Hotels, Villas, and Bed and Breakfasts

When it comes to choosing accommodation options in Sicily, travelers have several choices that cater to different needs, preferences, and budgets. Here are some more details on the three main options: hotels, villas, and bed and breakfasts:

Hotels:

Hotels are the most common accommodation option in Sicily and range from budget to luxury. There are numerous hotels in major cities, coastal towns, and rural areas. The facilities and amenities vary depending on the hotel's rating, but most hotels offer basic necessities such as private bathrooms, air conditioning, and Wi-Fi. Some hotels may also provide additional features such as swimming pools, spas, restaurants, and conference rooms. Prices vary depending on the location, time of year, and quality of the hotel.

Villas:

Villa rental is another popular accommodation option in Sicily, especially for families or larger groups of travelers. Villas provide more privacy and space than hotels and often come with a private pool, garden, and terrace. They are usually located in rural or coastal areas and offer stunning views of the surrounding landscape. Villas are self-catering, which means that guests can prepare their meals in a fully equipped kitchen or hire a chef for an additional fee. The cost of renting a villa depends on its location, size, and facilities.

Bed and Breakfasts:

Bed and Breakfasts (B&Bs) are small family-run establishments that offer a homely atmosphere and personalized service. They are usually located in the city center or in smaller towns and villages. B&Bs are ideal for travelers who prefer a more intimate and authentic experience. The rooms are often individually decorated, and breakfast is included in the price. Some B&Bs offer additional services such as guided tours, cooking classes, or airport transfers. Prices for B&Bs vary depending on the location, quality, and services provided.

Other Accommodation Options:

In addition to hotels, villas, and bed and breakfasts, there are several other accommodation options in Sicily that travelers can consider:

Hostels:

Hostels are a budget-friendly option for backpackers and solo travelers. They offer dormitory-style rooms with shared bathrooms and common areas. Some hostels also provide private rooms with en-suite bathrooms. Hostels are located in major cities and tourist destinations, and prices vary depending on the location and facilities.

Camping:

Camping is another affordable option for travelers who enjoy outdoor activities and nature. There are several campsites located in scenic areas across Sicily, offering tents or bungalows for rent.

Campsites usually provide basic facilities such as showers, toilets, and a communal kitchen.

Agriturismi:

Agriturismi are farmhouses that offer accommodation and meals to travelers. They are located in rural areas and provide a glimpse into traditional Sicilian life. Agriturismi offer comfortable rooms and apartments, as well as home-cooked meals made with local produce. They also offer activities such as hiking, horse riding, and farm tours.

Holiday Rentals:

Holiday rentals are self-catering apartments and houses that are available for short-term rent. They offer more space and privacy than hotels and are ideal for families or larger groups of travelers. Holiday rentals are located in cities, coastal towns, and rural areas, and prices vary depending on the location and facilities.

Choosing the Right Accommodation:

When choosing accommodation in Sicily, travelers should consider their budget, travel style, and preferences. It is recommended to research the location, facilities, and reviews of the accommodation before making a booking. Travelers should also check the cancellation policies and payment methods before confirming their reservation. It is also important to book in advance, especially during peak season, to secure the desired accommodation option.

Local Customs and Etiquette in Sicily

Greetings and Introductions: In Sicily, formal greetings and introductions are important. People should be addressed with titles and surnames, especially in business settings or with older people. In social situations, it is common to use first names with friends and acquaintances. When meeting someone for the first time, it is customary to shake hands, and for closer relationships, a kiss on each cheek may be exchanged. Eye contact is considered a sign of respect and honesty.

Cultural Traditions and Festivals: Sicily is rich in cultural traditions and festivals, many of which are religious in nature. Visitors should respect the customs and beliefs of the local people, especially during religious events. It is important to dress modestly and behave respectfully during these occasions.

Tipping and Service Charges: In restaurants and cafes, a service charge is usually included in the bill, but it is customary to leave a small tip if the service was good. The amount of the tip is generally 5-10% of the total bill. In other situations, such as hairdressers, taxi drivers or tour guides, tipping is not mandatory, but it is appreciated.

Dress Code and Appearance: Sicilians generally dress conservatively and modestly, especially in religious settings. Visitors should avoid wearing revealing clothing and opt for modest clothing that covers the shoulders and knees. Beachwear is only appropriate on the beach or by the pool. Sunglasses and hats are generally accepted in outdoor settings, but it is important to remove them when entering a church or other religious building.

Gift Giving and Souvenir Shopping: Gift giving is a common practice in Sicily, especially during festive occasions. It is important to choose gifts that reflect the recipient's interests or preferences. In general, it is not polite to open gifts in front of the giver. When shopping for souvenirs, visitors should be aware of the local craftsmanship and avoid buying counterfeit goods. Bargaining is common in street markets and small shops, but it should be done politely and respectfully.

Dining Etiquette: Sicilian cuisine is a blend of different cultures and traditions, and dining is an important social event. When dining in Sicily, it is important to wait to be seated, and to follow the host's lead when ordering and eating. Bread is served with most meals, and it is customary to use it to scoop up sauce and juices from the plate. It is considered rude to ask for additional condiments or to send food back to the kitchen. In formal dining situations, the host will pay for the meal, but it is polite to offer to pay or split the bill.

Family and Community: Family and community are highly valued in Sicilian culture, and visitors should respect and appreciate the importance of these relationships. It is common for families to live close together and for meals to be shared as a group. Visitors should avoid discussing controversial topics such as politics or religion, and should be respectful of different opinions and beliefs.

Gestures and Non-Verbal Communication: Non-verbal communication is an important aspect of Sicilian culture, and visitors should be aware of certain gestures that may have different meanings in other cultures. For example, making a circle with the thumb and forefinger is a vulgar gesture in Sicily. Eye contact is important, and avoiding it may be interpreted as a sign of disrespect. Physical touch is also common, and it is not uncommon for friends or acquaintances to embrace or touch each other during conversation.

Time Management: Sicilian time management is more relaxed than in other cultures, and punctuality is not always a top priority. Visitors should be prepared for delays and cancellations, and should be patient and flexible. It is also important to allow plenty of time for meals and social events, as these are often longer than in other cultures.

By being aware of these local customs and etiquette in Sicily, visitors can show their respect and appreciation for the local culture and traditions, and have a more enjoyable and rewarding travel experience.

Language and Communication Tips

Sicilian is a Romance language spoken in Sicily, but Italian is the official language used throughout Italy, including Sicily. Most people in Sicily speak Italian fluently, but you may also hear Sicilian dialect spoken in some parts of the island. Here are some tips to help you communicate effectively in Sicily:

Basic Phrases and Expressions:

Learning a few basic phrases and expressions in Italian can go a long way in making your trip to Sicily more enjoyable. Common phrases to know include greetings (buongiorno, buonasera), thank you (grazie), please (per favore), and excuse me (mi scusi). Additionally, knowing numbers, directions, and how to order food and drinks in Italian can be helpful.

Language Differences and Variations:

Sicilian has its own dialect, which is different from the Italian spoken on the mainland. While most people in Sicily speak Italian fluently, you may encounter some differences in vocabulary, pronunciation, and grammar. For example, in Sicilian, the word for "yes" is "occhiu" instead of the Italian "si". Additionally, Sicilian has some unique expressions and idioms that you may hear during your trip.

Non-Verbal Communication:

Non-verbal communication is an important aspect of communication in Sicily. Italians tend to use more gestures and facial expressions when communicating, and this is especially true in Sicily. Hand gestures are used to emphasize points, express emotion, and convey meaning. For example, the gesture of putting your fingers together and kissing them indicates something is delicious. Additionally, facial expressions can convey agreement, disagreement, or confusion.

Language Tools and Resources:

There are many language tools and resources available to help you communicate effectively in Sicily. Translation apps such as Google Translate or iTranslate can be useful for translating text or speaking phrases in Italian. Phrasebooks are another option for learning basic phrases and expressions. If you're interested in learning more about Italian, you can take language classes or use language learning apps like Duolingo or Rosetta Stone.

Additionally, when communicating with locals in Sicily, it is important to be respectful and polite. Italian culture places a strong emphasis on formalities and respect, so addressing people with the appropriate titles and using proper etiquette can go a long way in establishing a positive rapport.

When greeting someone, it is customary to use a formal greeting such as "buongiorno" (good morning) or "buonasera" (good evening) followed by the person's title and last name. For example, if you're speaking to someone named Giovanni, you would address him as "buongiorno, Signor Giovanni" or "buonasera, Signora Giovanni." Using titles such as "Signor" (Mr.) or "Signora" (Mrs.) is a sign of respect in Italian culture.

It's also important to be aware of cultural differences and customs when communicating with locals. For example, Italians tend to speak more loudly and use more hand gestures than other cultures, which may initially seem aggressive or confrontational to visitors. However, this is just a part of Italian communication style and is not meant to be offensive.

If you encounter a language barrier or are struggling to communicate, don't be afraid to ask for help. Many locals in Sicily speak English or may be able to point you in the direction of someone who does. Additionally, learning some basic Italian phrases and expressions before your trip can help you navigate everyday situations such as ordering food, buying tickets, or asking for directions.

In summary, knowing some basic Italian phrases, being aware of language differences, understanding non-verbal communication, and using language tools and resources can help you communicate effectively during your trip to Sicily.

Safety and Health Considerations

General Safety Tips:

- While Sicily is generally safe for travelers, it is still important to be aware of your surroundings, especially in tourist areas where pickpocketing and other petty crimes may occur.
- Avoid carrying large sums of cash or valuables on you when exploring the city, and be aware of your personal belongings at all times.
- It is also recommended to keep a copy of important documents such as passports, travel insurance, and emergency contact information in a safe place in case of theft or loss.

Natural Disasters and Emergency Preparedness:

- Sicily is prone to natural disasters such as earthquakes, volcanic eruptions, and floods, so it's important to be aware of potential hazards and have an emergency plan in place.

- It's a good idea to research the location you will be staying in advance, identify any potential risks and know the evacuation routes.
- In case of emergency, make sure you have an emergency kit with essential supplies such as a flashlight, food, water, and a first-aid kit.

Health Risks and Medical Care:

- While the risk of contracting illness while traveling to Sicily is relatively low, it is important to take necessary precautions to protect your health.
- Make sure to bring any necessary prescription medication with you and research the availability of medical facilities near your destination.
- If you have any pre-existing medical conditions, it's a good idea to consult with your doctor before traveling to ensure you have adequate treatment available.
- Travelers are also advised to stay hydrated and avoid consuming unfiltered water or undercooked food.

Travel Insurance:

- It's recommended to purchase travel insurance before your trip to Sicily to ensure that you are covered in case of unexpected illness, accidents, or travel delays.
- Make sure to review the terms and conditions of your policy carefully to understand what is covered and what is not.
- Additionally, check with your insurance provider to see if they have a preferred healthcare provider or hospital in Sicily.

Emergency Contacts and Assistance:

- In case of an emergency, it is important to know who to contact for help. The emergency number in Italy is 112 and can be used to request assistance from the police, fire department, or ambulance services.
- You can also reach out to your embassy or consulate for assistance if needed.
- It's a good idea to keep a list of emergency contacts with you at all times, including the contact information for your hotel or accommodation.

Other Safety and Health Considerations to Keep in Mind While Traveling to Sicily:

Road Safety:

Driving in Sicily can be challenging due to narrow roads, aggressive drivers, and limited parking. It is recommended to rent a smaller car and avoid driving in the city center.

Always wear your seatbelt and follow traffic laws to avoid accidents. Be aware of pedestrians and other vehicles, especially when driving on rural roads.

Beach Safety:

- Sicily has beautiful beaches, but it's important to be aware of potential hazards such as strong currents, jellyfish, and sunburn.
- Follow posted signs and warnings, swim only in designated areas with lifeguards on duty, and avoid swimming alone or at night.
- Always use sunscreen and wear protective clothing to prevent sunburn.

Animal Safety:

- Sicily has a significant population of stray cats and dogs. While they are generally friendly, it's best to avoid petting them or feeding them as they may carry diseases.
- Additionally, be aware of any wildlife you may encounter in rural areas such as snakes or wild boars.

Food and Water Safety:

- While Sicily has delicious cuisine, it's important to be aware of potential food and waterborne illnesses.
- Drink only bottled water and avoid ice made from tap water. Additionally, avoid raw or undercooked meats, seafood, and eggs to prevent food poisoning.
- If you have any food allergies or dietary restrictions, make sure to communicate this to restaurant staff to avoid any issues.

Tips for Staying Safe While Traveling:

- Always be aware of your surroundings and keep an eye on your belongings.
- Avoid carrying large amounts of cash or displaying expensive items like jewelry or cameras.
- If you're traveling alone, it's a good idea to let someone know where you're going and when you expect to return.
- If you're out at night, stick to well-lit areas and avoid walking alone in deserted areas.
- It's also important to be cautious when using public transportation, especially at night.

Taking necessary precautions and being aware of potential hazards can help ensure a safe and healthy trip to Sicily. By being prepared and informed, travelers can relax and enjoy all that this beautiful island has to offer.

Useful Phrases and Vocabulary

Basic Italian Phrases for Travelers

- Greetings and Introductions: "Ciao" (hello/goodbye), "Buongiorno" (good morning), "Buonasera" (good evening), "Come stai?" (how are you?)

- Ordering Food and Drink: "Per favore" (please), "Grazie" (thank you), "Un cappuccino, per favore" (a cappuccino, please), "Il conto, per favore" (the bill, please)
- Asking for Directions: "Dove si trova?" (where is it?), "Come si arriva?" (how do I get there?), "A destra/sinistra" (to the right/left), "Dritto" (straight ahead)

Sicilian Dialect and Expressions

- "Bedda" (beautiful), "Minniuni" (little one), "Cumpari" (friend), "Mizzica" (wow/exclamation of surprise), "Cazzu" (damn)

Note: Sicilian is a distinct dialect of Italian, and while it shares many similarities with standard Italian, it has its own unique vocabulary and expressions. It's worth noting that not all Sicilians speak Sicilian, and many also speak standard Italian.

Common Words and Phrases for Ordering Food and Drinks

- "Antipasto" (appetizer), "Primo piatto" (first course), "Secondo piatto" (second course), "Vino rosso/bianco" (red/white wine), "Birra" (beer)

Note: Sicilian cuisine is famous for its fresh seafood, pasta dishes, and pastries, so it's worth trying some local specialties while in Sicily.

Numbers and Currency Conversion

- "Uno, due, tre" (one, two, three), "Venti, trenta, quaranta" (20, 30, 40), "Euro" (euro), "Dollari" (dollars), "Cambio" (exchange rate)

Note: The official currency of Italy is the euro, and most places in Sicily accept credit cards. However, it's always a good idea to have some cash on hand for smaller purchases or in case of emergencies.

Transportation Terminology

- "Stazione" (station), "Biglietto" (ticket), "Treno" (train), "Autobus" (bus), "Aeroporto" (airport)

Note: While public transportation is available in Sicily, it's important to note that schedules and routes may vary, so it's best to check ahead of time to plan your trip accordingly. It's also worth noting that driving in Sicily can be challenging, especially in larger cities, so if you're planning to rent a car, be prepared for narrow streets, heavy traffic, and aggressive driving.

Emergency Contacts

If you're planning a trip to Sicily, it's important to know the emergency numbers for the area in case you need assistance while you're there. The following emergency numbers are important for visitors to Sicily to know:

Emergency Services - 112

The emergency services number in Sicily is 112. This number can be dialed from anywhere in the European Union and is designed to be used in case of an emergency. When you call this number, you will be connected to a multilingual operator who can dispatch the appropriate emergency services to your location. This number is available 24/7 and is free of charge.

Ambulance Services - 118

If you need an ambulance in Sicily, you can call 118. This number will connect you to the emergency medical services and they will dispatch an ambulance to your location. It's important to note that ambulance services in Sicily are only free for Italian citizens, and visitors may be charged for these services.

Fire Department - 115

If you need to report a fire in Sicily, you can call 115. This number will connect you to the fire department, and they will dispatch a fire truck to your location. The fire department in Sicily is well-equipped and trained to deal with a variety of emergencies, including fires and natural disasters.

Police - 113

If you need to report a crime or emergency situation in Sicily, you can call 113. This number will connect you to the police department, and they will dispatch officers to your location. It's important to note that the police in Sicily may not always speak English, so it's a good idea to have a basic understanding of Italian or to have a translator available.

Coast Guard - 1530

If you're in need of assistance on the water, you can call the Coast Guard in Sicily at 1530. This number will connect you to the maritime emergency services, and they will dispatch a rescue team or other appropriate services to your location. This number is specifically for emergencies on the water, and should not be used for non-emergency situations.

Roadside Assistance - 803116

If you're driving in Sicily and have a problem with your vehicle, you can call 803116 for roadside assistance. This number will connect you to the Italian automobile club, which provides roadside assistance services throughout the country. It's important to note that these services are not free and you will be charged for them.

Poison Control Center - 800.018.076

If you or someone you're with has ingested something poisonous or hazardous, you can call the Poison Control Center in Sicily at 800.018.076. This number is available 24/7 and can provide guidance on what to do in case of poisoning or exposure to a hazardous substance.

Animal Emergencies - 118

If you come across an injured animal or need to report an animal-related emergency in Sicily, you can call 118 to reach the emergency medical services for animals. They can dispatch a veterinarian or other appropriate services to assist with the situation.

Tourist Police - 0800.864.064

If you're a tourist in Sicily and need assistance with non-emergency situations such as lost documents, theft or other similar incidents, you can contact the Tourist Police at 0800.864.064. They can provide assistance in several languages, including English.

It's important to note that while these emergency numbers can provide vital assistance in case of an emergency, prevention is the best approach. It's recommended to take common sense precautions while traveling, such as staying in well-lit areas, keeping valuable items secure and avoiding dangerous situations.

In summary, being aware of the emergency numbers for visitors in Sicily can provide peace of mind while traveling. Keep these numbers readily available, and if possible, memorize them in case of an emergency. Stay safe and enjoy your trip to Sicily.

Transportation and Driving

Getting around Sicily can be an exciting adventure, but it's important to understand the various transportation options available and the best way to navigate the island's roads and highways.

Getting Around Sicily by Public Transportation

- Sicily has an extensive network of public transportation, including buses and trains.
- Buses are the most common form of public transportation and are operated by private companies that offer regular services between cities and towns.

- Trains are also available, with the main train line running along the eastern coast of the island from Messina to Siracusa.
- In addition, there are local city buses and trams in larger towns and cities.

Car Rentals and Driving Tips

- Car rentals are widely available throughout Sicily, and are a popular option for travelers who want more flexibility in their itinerary.
- It's important to note that driving in Sicily can be challenging, with narrow roads, steep hills, and tight corners.
- Traffic can also be congested in larger cities, especially during peak hours.
- It's recommended to rent a car with a GPS system, as the roads in Sicily can be confusing and difficult to navigate without one.
- Be sure to familiarize yourself with local traffic laws, speed limits, and road signs before embarking on a road trip.

Parking and Traffic Regulations

- Parking can be challenging in larger cities and tourist areas, with limited spaces and strict parking regulations.

- Be sure to park in designated areas and avoid parking in no-parking zones or blocking other vehicles.
- Traffic regulations are strictly enforced in Sicily, and traffic violations can result in fines and penalties.
- Keep in mind that driving under the influence of alcohol or drugs is illegal and can result in severe consequences.

Ferries and Boats to the Islands

- Sicily is surrounded by several smaller islands, such as the Aeolian Islands, Egadi Islands, and the Pelagie Islands.
- Ferries and boats operate regularly between the islands and the mainland, and can be a great way to explore more of Sicily's natural beauty.

Airports and Air Travel Information

- Sicily has two main airports: Falcone-Borsellino Airport in Palermo and Fontanarossa Airport in Catania.
- Both airports offer international and domestic flights, and have connections to other major cities in Italy and Europe.

- It's recommended to book flights in advance and check for any travel restrictions before traveling.

Useful apps and websites

Google Maps: This popular navigation app is an excellent tool for getting around Sicily. It provides real-time traffic updates, public transportation information, and detailed directions to your destination. You can also save maps offline to use when you don't have internet access.

Rome2rio: This website and app is an excellent resource for planning your transportation in Sicily. It provides a comprehensive overview of your options, including flights, trains, buses, ferries, and more. You can compare prices, schedules, and travel times to find the best option for your needs.

Duolingo: If you're interested in learning a bit of Italian before your trip to Sicily, Duolingo is a great place to start. This language-learning app is fun, easy to use, and free. You can learn vocabulary, grammar, and conversational Italian at your own pace.

Airbnb: This website and app allows you to find unique and affordable accommodations in Sicily. You can search for apartments, villas, and even castles to rent, often at a lower price than traditional hotels. Airbnb also provides a local experience, allowing you to live like a Sicilian and explore the area like a resident.

Tripadvisor: This website and app is a great resource for researching things to do in Sicily. You can read reviews from other travelers, browse photos, and find recommendations for restaurants, attractions, and activities. You can also book tours and activities directly through the site.

Google Translate: This app is a useful tool for communicating with locals in Sicily. It can translate text, speech, and images in real-time, making it easy to understand signs, menus, and conversations. You can even download offline language packs to use when you don't have internet access.

Skyscanner: This website and app is a great resource for finding affordable flights to Sicily. You can search for flights from your home airport to Sicily, compare prices, and find the best deals. Skyscanner also allows you to set price alerts, so you'll be notified when fares drop.

XE Currency: This app provides real-time exchange rates for over 180 currencies, making it easy to convert your money to euros before your trip. You can also use the app to track your expenses and stay within your budget while in Sicily.

Trenitalia: If you're planning to travel by train in Sicily, Trenitalia is the primary railway operator in Italy. The website and app allows you to book tickets, check schedules, and get information about train stations and services. You can also save your tickets on your phone and avoid the hassle of printing.

TripIt: This app is a great tool for organizing your itinerary and travel plans in one place. You can forward your confirmation emails for flights, hotels, and activities to TripIt, and it will create a master itinerary for you. You can also add notes, maps, and other information to make your trip more organized.

By using these and other useful apps and websites, you can make the most of your time in Sicily and have a stress-free travel experience. However, it's important to note that not all of these apps may work in the same way in Sicily as they do in other parts of the world, so it's a good idea to research and test them before your trip.

Conclusion

In conclusion, the Sicily Travel Guide is a comprehensive and invaluable resource for anyone planning to explore this beautiful island in the Mediterranean. From the coast to the countryside, this guide has covered all the essential information and insider tips needed to experience the best of Sicily.

As you have learned, Sicily is a land of contrasts and beauty, from the stunning beaches and seaside towns to the ancient archaeological sites and art-filled cities. It is a place where culinary delights abound, and where cultural traditions and heritage are celebrated with passion and enthusiasm.

With this guide in hand, you will be able to navigate Sicily with ease, uncover hidden gems, and immerse yourself in the island's rich history, culture, and lifestyle. You will discover the best places to stay, the most delicious food to eat, and the most fascinating sights to see. And you will do all of this with confidence and ease, knowing that you have the best possible guidance at your fingertips.

In short, the Sicily Travel Guide is not just a guidebook, but a gateway to an unforgettable adventure in one of the most fascinating destinations in the world. So pack your bags, grab your copy of the guide, and get ready to experience all that Sicily has to offer. We guarantee that you won't be disappointed.

Printed in Great Britain
by Amazon

21190044R00098